DAVID
Seeking God's Heart

BETH MOORE

LifeWay Press®
Nashville, Tennessee

© 2001 LifeWay Press®
Reprinted 2003, 2005, 2006, 2007, 2008, 2010, 2012, June 2014, Oct. 2015

ISBN: 978-0-6330-1734-7
Item 00105978

Dewey Decimal Classification Number: 248.83
Subject Heading: TEENAGERS—ATTITUDES \ ADOLESCENCE \ DAVID, KING OF ISRAEL

Printed in the United States of America

Student Ministry Publishing
LifeWay Resources
One LifeWay Plaza
Nashville, TN 37234-0144

We believe that the Bible has God for its author; salvation for its
end; and truth, without any mixture of error, for its matter and that
all Scripture is totally true and trustworthy. The 2000 statement of
The Baptist Faith and Message is our doctrinal guideline.

Cover Photography: A.S.A.P./Caro Nalbandian

CONTENTS

Meet Beth Moore

Beth Moore realized at the age of 18 that God was claiming her future for full-time ministry. While she was sponsoring a cabin of sixth graders at a missions camp, God unmistakably acknowledged that she would work for Him. There Beth gave all parts of her life to the Lord she had loved since childhood. However, she had a problem: although she knew she was "wonderfully made," she was "fearfully" without talent. She hid behind closed doors to discover whether a beautiful singing voice had miraculously developed, but the results were tragic. She returned to her piano from which years of practice resulted in joyless noise. Finally accepting that the only remaining alternative was missions work in a foreign country, she waited. Nothing happened.

Still confident of God's calling, Beth finished her degree at Southwest Texas State University, where she fell in love with Keith. After they married in December 1978, God added three blessings: Amanda, Melissa, and Michael.

As if putting together puzzle pieces one at a time, God filled Beth's path with supportive persons who saw something in her she could not. God used individuals like Marge Caldwell, John Bisagno, and Jeannette Cliff George to help Beth discover gifts of speaking, teaching, and writing. Now years after her first speaking engagement, those gifts have spread all over the world. Her joy and excitement in Christ are contagious; her deep love for the Savior, obvious; her style of speaking, electric.

Beth's ministry is grounded in and fueled by her service at her home fellowship, First Baptist Church, Houston, Texas, where she serves on the pastor's council and teaches a Sunday School class attended by more than two hundred women. Beth believes that her calling is to guide believers to love and live God's Word. *A Heart Like His: Seeking the Heart of God through a Study of David*—which is the basis for *David: Seeking God's Heart*—grew from her burning desire that believers experience greater intimacy with God.

Beth loves the Lord, loves to laugh, and loves to be with His people. Her life is full of activity, but one commitment remains constant: counting all things but loss for the excellence of knowing Christ Jesus, the Lord. (See Phil. 3:8.)

Introduction

Welcome to a study of *David: Seeking God's Heart*. I am thrilled you've chosen to take this journey through Scripture with me! We have quite an expedition before us as we tour the pastures, caves, and palace of one of the most well-known figures in history—King David.

We will quickly discover David's multi-faceted personality. Our responses to his experiences will likely be as extreme as he was. He will make us laugh and possibly cry. He will delight us, and he will disappoint us. He will make us want to be just like him at times and nothing like him at others.

The life and times of David will cause us to have many responses, but boredom will not likely be one of them! He is sure to capture your interest, if you let him. And God is sure to change your heart, if you let Him.

Get Ready

Getting prepared for a study of David is like getting ready for a tornado. Get your Bible, this book, and a pen. Find a quiet place where you can study, and hold on for dear life!

These pages will highlight the best and the worst of humanity. David lived thousands of years ago, yet he dealt with many of the issues that plague God's people today. If you've ever had doubts, fought temptations, struggled with the inconsistency of saying one thing and doing another, fallen into sin, suffered losses, or hurt deeply over family problems, this Bible study is for you. (If you haven't, you may need to check your pulse!)

Set Your Pace

David: Seeking God's Heart is a six-week Bible study that will take you through virtually every twist and turn of David's life as a shepherd, a refugee, and a king. Each chapter contains enough biblical truth, drama, and even humor for you to read throughout the week. Although you will find natural breaks in each chapter, you can divide the reading and personal assignments any way you like. A section of each chapter may take you 15 minutes or 45 minutes to complete, depending on how much material you decide to tackle. Completing each week's assignment is crucial for you to benefit from the study.

Go to the Source

Because the study takes you verse by verse through Scripture, it reads like an epic of one man's life. Within each chapter you will find points of Discovery that deal with the persons and events in the life of David.

In addition to the points of Discovery, you will find opportunities for personal reflection. Each Meditation will help you relate the events to your own life.

You will also be asked to complete reading assignments and various types of learning activities. You may find multiple-choice questions, true/false activities, fill-in-the-blank statements, creative thinking exercises, or straightforward questions that you will answer in your own words. Respond to the questions in each chapter. This Bible study delves into several personal subjects. At times, your heart may overflow with the desire to share what God is doing through the study of David. Other times, you may want to keep God's very personal work between the two of you.

Scripture: Historical Biography and "Autobiography"

Each chapter highlights Scripture that best represents the chapter's theme. You will read many of the Psalms, almost half of which are considered to have been written by David himself. You will also occasionally be asked to write a Scripture to emphasize what God's Word is saying to you.

Journaling

The biography of 1 and 2 Samuel along with the "autobiography" of the Psalms will challenge you to reflect on your own life story. God wants to speak to you personally through His Word. We do not study Scripture to increase our head knowledge. We want God to change our hearts and lives.

Throughout each chapter I encourage you to ask two questions: In what ways do you believe God is speaking directly to you? What is your response to Him?

In addition to the response space in this book you may want to keep a journal to record your "overflow" thoughts. Journaling is a wonderful way to focus on God's activity in and around you. A small notebook will do. Writing things down will help you remember and reflect on how God specifically speaks to you. Each time He speaks to you, make a fresh commitment to Him. Your life will be transformed.

The Small-Group Experience

The best way to study *David: Seeking God's Heart* is in a group. You are more likely to complete this study if you enjoy the benefits of a weekly discussion group. As a member of a group, you will meet regularly for accountability.

Your small group will discuss key points from each chapter. Your group will also spend time sharing and praying together. However, you will never be expected to share anything personal in the group. Share only what you are comfortable talking about.

Make the group meetings a priority. Hebrews 11:6 states, "Anyone who comes to him must believe that he exists and that he rewards those who earnestly seek him" (NIV). This study offers you the opportunity to earnestly seek God.

A Final Word

This study takes courage, my friend. I have made specific adjustments in my personal life, as a direct result of God's direction studying the life of David. You cannot be confronted by God's Word day after day and refuse to change. You will either shut the book or allow God to change you. Allow Him to let every word mold you just like *David: Seeking God's Heart!*

Chapter One

OVERCOMING GIANTS

God is greater than any situation that
you will ever encounter.

Scripture

"Nothing can hinder
the Lord from saving,
whether by many or
by few" (1 Sam. 14:6).

We will encounter many colorful personalities in these six chapters. Our journey begins with Saul and Jonathan, a father and son who will have a tremendous impact on David. Saul was the reigning king of Israel. Jonathan was his son, the heir apparent to the throne. Our study begins in the middle of the reign of King Saul, the people's choice.

Take time to read 1 Samuel 8–11. You will discover that Saul not only was chosen with the wrong motive, he often reigned with the wrong motive! "You acted foolishly,"

Discovery

You will discover that God always brings good—even from the worst motives.

Samuel said. "You have not kept the command the Lord your God gave you; if you had, he would have established your kingdom over Israel for all time. But now your kingdom will not endure; the Lord has sought out a man after his own heart and appointed him leader of his people, because you have not kept the Lord's command" (1 Sam. 13:13-14).

Good news and bad news erupted from Samuel's prophecy. The bad news was that the kingdom of Israel's first monarch would not endure. Saul had a bad habit of compromising the commands of God. The king refused to wait on the Lord, trust in His Word, and follow His directions. Saul proved that a person can have good characteristics without having good character! The good news was: "The Lord has sought out a man after his own heart." This is Scripture's first description of the most beloved king in Israel's history: David, the son of Jesse! God used this very description to compel my desire to write this study.

What do you understand the expression "a person after God's own heart" to mean?

A person after what god wants.

Meet Jonathan, son of King Saul, a man quite different from his father. Jonathan became dear to David and is likely to become dear to us.

Read 1 Samuel 14:1-23. Describe the relationship between Jonathan and his armor-bearer. Be specific. Parthers and friends because they took down some people

First Samuel 14:6 is a powerful statement. Write your own paraphrase of the following portion of Scripture: "Perhaps the Lord will act in our behalf. Nothing can hinder the Lord from saving, whether by many or by few."

Jonathan and his armor-bearer were impressive men and worthy examples.

1. Jonathan's perception of the Lord's ways. His keen perception of the Lord certainly did not come from his father, because Jonathan's understanding exceeds that of Saul. Jonathan had his own relationship with the Lord, completely separate from his father's. Jonathan made two profound statements in verse 6:
- "*Perhaps* the Lord will act in our behalf."
- "*Nothing* can hinder the Lord from saving, whether by many or by few."

Consider how these statements reveal Jonathan's perception of God's ways: Jonathan knew the Lord could save, no matter who or how many were fighting the battle. In fact, he knew that if God chose to save, nothing could hinder him! His faith in God's strength and determination was solid: God could do anything. His only question was whether or not God would choose to do it through them that day. Reread Jonathan's words: "*Perhaps the Lord will act in our behalf.*" He *knew* God could do it; he didn't know if He *would*. Whether or not He did, Jonathan understood God's response to be based on sovereignty, not weakness. Jonathan's attitude reminds me of several other young men also facing the strong possibility of death.

Read Romans 10:17 and fill in the diagram below, with the two components which lead to faith.

_____hearing_____ ➔ _____hearing the word_____ ➔ **FAITH**

Two critical elements result in faith: the message of Christ and our experience of hearing the message.

Jonathan was not the only impressive individual. Let's look at the significant example of his armor-bearer.

2. *The armor-bearer's commitment to Jonathan's authority.* As you described their relationship earlier you probably noted the armor-bearer's constant obedience to Jonathan's commands. You can draw a wonderful parallel between the armor-bearer and a Christian.

Read Ephesians 6:10-13. In these verses, what is God's command to us?
❑ Stand and watch the salvation of the Lord.
☑ Put on the whole armor of God.
❑ Ignore the enemy and he will have to flee.

What is the stated purpose of the command to put on the armor?
❑ We will intimidate our enemy.
❑ We keep from getting slaughtered.
☑ We can take our stand against the devil's schemes.

Whose armor are we supposed to put on? _god's armor_

We are God's present *armor-bearers*. We're not just to carry it. We are to put it on. I want you to see just how much we compare to Jonathan's armor-bearer. Take a good look at the word *struggle* in Ephesians 6:12. The Greek word *pale* means, "A wrestling, struggle or hand-to-hand combat. It was used of the wrestling of athletes and the hand-to-hand combat of soldiers.... It denoted the struggle between individual combatants in distinction from an entire military campaign."[1] Our "struggle" against our enemy is a very personal battle. *Pale* does not describe a corporate battle. It describes a struggle which involves only ourselves—the One whose armor we bear—and our enemy!

Jonathan's armor-bearer set a wonderful example. Look again at 1 Samuel 14 and let's draw some applications that may help us in our battle:
• The armor-bearer listened carefully to Jonathan's instructions. To be victorious, we must also listen carefully to the instructions of the One whose armor we bear. The Sword of the Spirit, the Word of God, will both prepare us and protect us!

Our "struggle" against our enemy is a very personal battle ... a struggle which involves only ourselves—the One whose armor we bear—and our enemy!

Meditation

Pray a brief prayer regarding any desire you have to be with God "heart and soul."

We would avoid our spiritual battles if we could, but our Master is always careful to lead the way.

• The *New International Version* described Jonathan's armor-bearer as being with his master "heart and soul" (v. 7).

What did the armor-bearer mean by pledging himself to Jonathan "heart and soul"?

_____

_____

How often do you believe you are with God "heart and soul"?
❑ often
❑ occasionally
☑ rarely
❑ I don't believe I've ever really been with God "heart and soul."

• The armor-bearer *followed* behind Jonathan. His master *led* him into battle. He did not choose the battle. Jonathan made sure he went ahead of the armor-bearer so that he could take the blows of the enemy. When we received Christ as Savior, we enlisted in an army. We would avoid our spiritual battles if we could, but our Master is always careful to lead the way. We must always "climb up" after Him. Notice that 1 Samuel 14:13 states, "The Philistines fell before Jonathan, and his armor-bearer followed and killed behind him." Our enemy will fall before our God. We are only deadly to the enemy when we go *behind* Him.

Read 1 Samuel 14:24-52. How did Saul inadvertently put his army in jeopardy? Choose one.
☑ He forced his men to fast.
❑ He forced them to settle in enemy territory.
❑ He forced them to fight an enemy too powerful for them.

According to verses 31-33, what happened as a result of their "fast"? Check all that apply.
❑ They could not face their enemy.
❑ They discovered supernatural strength.
☑ They became exhausted.
☑ They ended up eating the wrong things.

What tragedy almost resulted from Saul's selfish command? Choose one.
☑ Jonathan was almost put to death.
❑ David nearly lost his life.
❑ Saul was nearly captured by the Philistines.
❑ The men almost died of starvation.

Note an important fact about fasting. God, not man, must call "fasts." Fasting called by God will result in added strength, not depleted strength. Fasting for any other reason works against us rather than for us. Fasting is a wonderful and highly effective discipline of God, but we must follow His instruction for fasting so we will be strengthened rather than weakened in our battles.

According to 1 Kings 19:7-8, what did God command Elijah to do because of his fear and exhaustion at the prospect of facing Jezebel? *Eat some food or you will die halfway through the journey.*

People often "fast" for the wrong reasons. We may call it "dieting" and it often violates the bounds of nutritional eating. Such "fasting" can lead to a form of starvation.

Have you ever withheld food from yourself for a considerable length of time when it wasn't God's idea? ❑ Yes ❑ No If your answer is yes, in the margin describe how you felt and what eventually happened.

Hasty, self-centered vows can cost us. Not only did Saul's army end up sinning against God, but Saul could easily have lost his son. God tried to teach Saul a serious lesson that day. Saul's pride could have caused him to keep a foolish vow. Better to repent than to add foolishness to foolishness.

In each battle we've studied, we've seen evidence that God is for us in battle, not against us. He wants us fortified before our enemy with faith like Jonathan, obedience like the armor-bearer, and proper fuel like Saul's army should have received.

❧❧

W e now witness a confrontation between King Saul and Samuel the prophet. The confrontation speaks to us as we consider our response to God's instructions. The Scriptures we will read will likely leave quite an impression on you.

Read 1 Samuel 15:1-35. In one sentence write what you believe is the theme of this chapter. _____

What is the most shocking or troublesome verse or statement in this chapter? Why?
_____

Which one of the following words best describes God's response to Saul's actions in verses 11 and 12?
❑ fury ❑ jealousy ❑ indifference ❑ bitterness ☑ grief ❑ guilt

According to verse 11, how did Samuel respond to Saul's disobedience? *cried all night*

God is for us in battle, not against us.

Scripture

Samuel replied: "Does the Lord delight in burnt offerings and sacrifices as much as in obeying the voice of the Lord? To obey is better than sacrifice, and to heed is better than the fat of rams" (1 Sam. 15:22).

Discovery

You will discover that obedience is better than sacrifice.

When Samuel went to meet Saul, he had gone to Carmel to set up a monument in his own honor. What insight can you gain into Saul's heart based on his trip to Carmel? he's having pride.

When Samuel confronted Saul what reason did Saul give for sparing the livestock according to verse 15?
☐ The livestock could provide food and clothing for the Israelites.
☑ The best livestock was spared to offer them as sacrifices to God.
☐ The livestock of the Amalekites was healthier than Israel's livestock.
☐ The livestock would be an impressive addition to Israel's assets.

Which one of the following statements most reflects Saul's attitude according to verses 20 and 21?
☑ Partial obedience is still obedience.
☐ God doesn't make His instructions clear enough to be followed.
☐ God's ideas are good unless a better one comes along.
☐ Other: _____

What is God saying in verse 22? _____

Our God seems so unlike the One who ordered an entire people destroyed, doesn't He? If God is love, light, and cannot tempt us to sin, we must need to know more to adequately evaluate 1 Samuel 15. To understand the grave command of God, we need to know the history of the Amalekites. They were the first people to attack the Israelites after their exodus (Ex. 17:8-16). After initial defeat, they attacked Israel again, this time forcing them back into the Sinai wilderness (Num. 14:39-45).

Read carefully the words of Moses to the Israelites in Deuteronomy 25:17-19. Note everything you learn about the Amalekites by completing the following sentences:
They met the Israelites on their way out of Egypt and Amalek
They had no fear of god
The Israelites would eventually blot out their memory
The Israelites must not forget

God is sovereign. He owes us no explanation as to why He desired for this entire population to be exterminated. However, we can assume they were a vile and godless people, because God is merciful and compassionate.

Look up Jonah 3:10; 4:1-2 and Ezekiel 33:11. What do these verses say about God's mercy on wicked people? _____

The passages from Jonah and Ezekiel clearly demonstrate God's desire to forgive and rescue all people from evil. From all the Bible states about the Amalekites, I assume that they rejected every opportunity to repent of evil and turn to God.

Saul made some serious presumptions. He kept King Agag alive, not to spare his life out of mercy, but to present him as a trophy. He did not slaughter the sheep and cattle for the same reason: he saved the best to make himself look better. Verse 9 ends with a sad commentary on Saul's actions: "These they were unwilling to destroy completely, but everything that was despised and weak they totally destroyed."

Several breaches in character become evident in this dramatic chapter.

1. Saul was arrogant. If we needed any further proof of Saul's pride and audacity, verse 12 certainly provides it. Saul went directly to Carmel and built a monument to himself. A short time later Samuel reminded Saul that God had anointed him king over Israel when he was small in his own eyes.

Which words describe what Samuel meant by the term, "small in your own eyes"?
☑ **self-conscious**   ☐ **low self-esteem**   ☐ **self-denying**   ☐ **humble**

Of these four answers, circle the one(s) that describes a positive, Christ-honoring form of being "small in your own eyes."

For Saul being "small in his own eyes" meant being self-conscious. We could probably guess that his self-esteem was inappropriately low. The Bible encourages self-denial and humility as positive ways of recognizing our "smallness" before God.

What are some ways you could keep your heart humble before God? _____
_____
_____

2. Saul refused to take responsibility for his actions. Saul first excused himself for disobeying God by claiming he spared the best of the sheep and cattle for a sacrifice to the Lord. Amazing, isn't it? Today a person might claim the reason he robbed a bank was to give a greater tithe and offering to the Lord. Believe it or not, we can sometimes use God as our excuse for disobedience, too. A girl may deliberately disobey and deceive godly parents to go to a party because she is certain God's will is for her to be a positive witness at the social event of the year. A guy may explain his social drinking as God's way for him to be accepted by and be a light to the other guys on the team.

Can you think of another example of disobedience in God's name? _____
_____
_____

Saul not only tried to use God as his excuse for disobedience, he also claimed he was afraid of and gave in to the people (v. 24). The king of Israel with God on his side scared

Believe it or not, we can sometimes use God as our excuse for disobedience.

Meditation

Reflect on a time in your life when you knew God was humbling you so that He could more fully use you.

My Temptations

_____
_____
_____
_____
_____
_____
_____
_____
_____
_____
_____
_____
_____
_____
_____
_____
_____
_____

of his people? When we've done something wrong or foolish, we find shouldering the responsibility difficult, don't we? At times we are all tempted to blame someone else when we've blown it. I wonder if the outcome might have been different if Saul simply had admitted he made a wrong choice. We have lots of opportunities for good choices. Our first choice should be to obey God. Our second choice should be to take responsibility for poor decisions when we make them. Ask God to make you keenly aware of times when you try to "pass the buck" instead of taking responsibility for something you should or shouldn't have done. Thank God He can change our nature! Don't get discouraged. Awareness is the first step to change!

3. *Saul minimized the seriousness of disobedience.* In verse 23, Samuel compares rebellion to the sin of divination or witchcraft. The comparison seems puzzling until we consider that rebellion is a means by which we attempt to set the course of our futures. We try to choose our own futures by our independent actions. Divination attempts to foretell or sway the future. In the same verse, God likens arrogance to the evil of idolatry. When we are arrogant, who becomes God in our lives?

The chapter concludes with a frightening scene. Samuel hacked King Agag to pieces. Samuel's actions were not in haste, nor did he approach Saul and say "I told you so." Samuel acted in obedience.

What did you learn about Samuel's heart in verses 11 and 35? _____
_____
_____

> **Saul learned that obedience was better than sacrifice. Samuel learned that sometimes obedience *is* the sacrifice.**

Scripture

> "The Lord does not look at the things man looks at. Man looks at the outward appearance, but the Lord looks at the heart" (1 Sam. 16:7).

Perhaps Samuel's heart was the reason God used him as He did. Samuel's heart never grew cold and condemning. God allowed Samuel to be emotionally involved but enabled him to maintain objectivity so that he could "speak the truth in love" (Eph. 4:15). Saul learned that obedience was better than sacrifice. Samuel learned that sometimes obedience *is* the sacrifice.

I love to discover new truths through Scripture. I also love reading the familiar passages over and over again. Perhaps the following passage of Scripture is one that you are familiar. If so, I know you won't mind looking at it again.

Read 1 Samuel 16:1-13. What assignment did God give the prophet Samuel in verse 1? to get a king
_____
_____

Why was Samuel initially reluctant to go to Bethlehem?
❑ His health was failing.   ❑ He felt unworthy.
☑ He was afraid Saul would kill him.   ❑ His sons were unruly.

14

Samuel initially assumed God's choice was Eliab, Jesse's oldest son. Based on God's response to Samuel, why do you think Samuel chose Eliab? _____
_____
_____

When Samuel asked Jesse if he had any other sons, Jesse answered, "There is still the youngest ... but he is tending the sheep."

Which of the following words describe Jesse's youngest son?
❏ rugged ☑ ruddy ☑ handsome ❏ tall ❏ strong ❏ shy

Write the Lord's commandment to Samuel in verse 12. _____
_____
_____
_____

How did the Spirit of God make Himself known in the life of David from the time He came upon him?
☑ in power ❏ in glory ❏ in authority ❏ in zeal ❏ in countenance

Samuel's stubbornness is funny to me. Notice his response to Jesse once he learned that Jesse had one more son. "Send for him; we will not sit down until he arrives." He knew how to get them moving! Don't forget how everyone trembled when he arrived in Bethlehem. No one wanted to have the prophet of God drop by unannounced!

David, a young teenager, arrived on the scene with no idea what awaited him. He was handsome with a reddish complexion and no doubt smelled like sheep. He obviously was not his own father's first choice nor would he have been Samuel's. The prophet assumed God's choice was Eliab. This choice made the most sense. He was the eldest son. He looked like a king.

God taught Samuel a very important lesson. "Man looks at the outward appearance, but the Lord looks at the heart." He reminded Samuel that the human mind tends to make assumptions based on appearances. God's choices don't always make sense to us.

When my oldest brother was born, my mother wholeheartedly gave him to the Lord. By the time he was five years old, he was showing remarkable signs of musical talent. He had earned many honors by the time he was in high school and had developed impressive leadership skills. He earns a very good living as a conductor and composer in the secular entertainment world. My big brother has always been a hero to me. He not only is the most talented person I've ever known, he is one of the dearest.

I came along in the family as the fourth of five children and never could find my niche. I couldn't sing or play an instrument. I was not outstanding at anything. Strangely, God heard my mother's devotion and He honored her desire to give a child back to the Lord

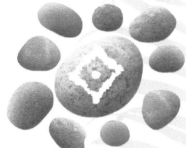

Discovery

You will discover that although God's choices are not always clear and at sometimes may seem confusing to us, He is sovereign. God is always in control.

David, a young teenager, arrived on the scene with no idea what awaited him.

God's choices don't always make sense to us, but they are never random.

Meditation

Can you think of a time when God's obvious choice for you did not make sense based on outward appearances?

to serve Him. For reasons I will never know, He did not choose the one who made the most sense. He chose the one who made the least—me. I can't even tell you what He saw in my heart worth using except that He knew in advance I would say yes.

God's choices don't always make sense to us but they are never random. A closer look at David sheds light on why God may have chosen him. The first consideration is his genealogy. Let's do a little research.

The Old Testament Book of Ruth tells of a woman and her mother-in-law after the deaths of their husbands. Ruth is not only one of the most important women in Hebrew history, she also had a special relationship to David.

Read Ruth 4:13-17. Who was Ruth in relation to David?
☑ **David's great-grandmother** ❑ **David's grandmother** ❑ **David's aunt**
❑ **None of the above**

Look at Matthew 1:1-17. Whose genealogy is listed? _Jesus_

What two titles is Christ given in verse 1?
☑ **the son of David** ❑ **the son of God** ❑ **the son of man** ☑ **the son of Abraham**

The genealogy David and Christ shared was significant. In verse 3, you can see that both David and Christ were descendants of Judah, one of the sons of Jacob. In the prophecy Jacob spoke over Judah, he told him that "The scepter will not depart from Judah, nor the ruler's staff from between his feet" (Gen. 49:10). You see, David was not a random choice. He was one of the most important figures in the genealogy of Christ, the Lion of the tribe of Judah (Rev. 5:5).

I never fail to be encouraged by Christ's heritage. Besides Jesus, you will not find on the list the name of any other perfect character.

How do you respond to the fact that the only perfect person on Christ's genealogy is Christ Himself? _____
_____
_____
_____
_____

In many ways David's life foreshadowed details of Christ's life. God illustrated the unknown about the Messiah through the known about David. David was not divine nor perfect, as we will quickly discover, but God will use him to teach us truths about the One who is. I think you'll enjoy knowing that the name Jesse is a "personal name meaning, 'man.' "[2] Christ referred to Himself as the "Son of Man" more than any other title. He asked His disciples, "Who do people say the Son of Man is?" (Matt. 16:13). Isn't it interesting that David, King of Israel, who often pointed to Jesus was also technically the "Son of Man"?

David's occupation also made him a candidate for kingship. At first glance, few similarities appear between a shepherd and a king, but we will discover that David received invaluable experience keeping sheep. Psalm 78:70-72 states: "He chose David his servant and took him from the sheep pens; from tending the sheep he brought him to be the shepherd of his people Jacob, of Israel his inheritance. And David shepherded them with integrity of heart; with skillful hands he led them."

Did God call David in spite of the fact that he was a common shepherd? _____
_____
_____

If you have a part-time job or other responsibility for which you earn money, what occupational skills do you use? _____

Have you ever felt that your occupational skills were useless in areas of service to God? ☑ Yes ☑ No

Can you think of any ways God can use or has used you because of your skills and not just in spite of them? Yo _____
_____
_____
_____

> **Few things seem less spiritual than keeping a bunch of smelly sheep, yet God used David's skills for eternal purposes.**

Few things seem less spiritual than keeping a bunch of smelly sheep, yet God used David's skills for eternal purposes. Those who went to "fetch him" (KJV) could not have easily torn David from his sheep. You can be certain he did not leave his sheep shepherd-less. Someone had to stay in his place while he ran home. Later we see evidence that he returned to his sheep after receiving an anointing he tried to understand (v. 19). When David arrived at home, Samuel saw that he was "ruddy, with a fine appearance and handsome features." Still, Samuel did not move. He had already made a mistake based on appearances. Then God said, "Rise and anoint him; he is the one."

Look at 1 Samuel 16:13 and complete the verse: "Samuel took the horn of oil and anointed him in the presence of his brothers, and from that day on the spirt came upon him _____
_____

As we study the life of this shepherd boy, we will no doubt see the Holy Spirit's power again and again. Samuel stood before a young lad and with awe and reverence poured the oil on his head. Although the oil surely blurred David's vision, God's vision was crystal clear. God had said, "I will send thee to Jesse the Bethlehemite: for I have provided me a king among his sons" (1 Sam. 16:1, KJV). The Hebrew word for *provided* is *ra'ah*. It means "to see, to look at, view, inspect, regard, to perceive; … to feel; to experience."[3] Second Chronicles 16:9 says, "the eyes of the Lord run to and fro throughout the whole earth, to show Himself strong on behalf of those whose heart is loyal to Him" (NKJV).

Scripture

"I have seen a son of Jesse of Bethlehem who knows how to play the harp. He is a brave man and a warrior. He speaks well and is a fine-looking man. And the Lord is with him" (1 Sam. 16:18).

Discovery

You will discover that Jesus set an example of true manhood and true womanhood. No greater person exists than one who is both tender and strong.

That day so many years ago, the eyes of the Lord looked throughout the whole earth and fell upon an obscure little village called Bethlehem. There He found a heart—one like His own. He found a heart that was tender toward little lost sheep, and He showed Himself strong on behalf of that heart, just like He promised.

We have sat in the audience and witnessed the anointing of a man after God's own heart. Now we focus our attention on the remaining verses which complete the bridge connecting the lives of King Saul and young David.

Read 1 Samuel 16:13-23. Verses 13 and 14 tell of two contrasting activities of the Holy Spirit. Describe the two activities of the Spirit and the results that came from them. _____
_____
_____
_____

How did David come into Saul's service? _____
_____
_____

What was David's first position under Saul's authority?
❑ servant ☑ armor-bearer ❑ guard ❑ cup-bearer ❑ door-keeper

List every description you discover about David in verse 18. A man of war, the lord was with him _____
_____

What effect did David's music have on the tormented king?
❑ helped him sleep ☑ felt better ☑ evil spirit left
❑ all of the above

The Holy Spirit had a different relationship with people before Christ died on the cross. Now His Spirit lives in all believers (Rom. 8:9). Before Calvary, the Holy Spirit worked to empower specific types of service rather than to bring a new relationship with God through salvation. Less than 100 people in the Old Testament were ever characterized by the Holy Spirit being on or in them. The Holy Spirit came on only those who were being empowered for specific tasks or positions.

Another important contrast can be drawn between the Holy Spirit in the Old Testament and in the New Testament. Saul's experience demonstrates that the Holy Spirit could depart from a person. After the atoning death of Christ, the Spirit comes to establish a new and permanent relationship with the believer. The Gospel of John offers believers assurance concerning the gift of the Holy Spirit.

Read John 14:16-17 and explain the assurance we now have. _____

_____

_____

Have you ever been afraid that you might have done something to make the Holy Spirit leave you? ❏ Yes ☑ No

Read Romans 8:38-39. How do these verses encourage you in your relationship to God through Jesus Christ? _____

_____

> **The Spirit comes to establish a new and permanent relationship with the believer.**

Saul did not have the same assurance we have of the continuing presence of God's Spirit. We have nothing to compare to Saul's experience. I can imagine nothing more horrifying than the Holy Spirit leaving me. Unfortunately, the departure of the Holy Spirit did not just leave Saul empty. It left a door open to evil.

Although David's anointing did not end Saul's reign as king, it marked the end of the power and favor of God on him. Just as God prepared Abraham for many years before he was ready to assume his position, God thoroughly prepared David for his role as king long before he was crowned.

The exit of the Holy Spirit left Saul open to the torment of an evil spirit. If he had been a man of character, Saul might have cooperated with God to add David to his royal ranks through less painful means, but Saul had already proved himself to be self-centered and rebellious. God used Saul's selfishness to bring David to the royal courts.

God is sovereign. He allowed the evil spirit to torment Saul. He knows what methods will work to bring about His will. David had to be summoned to the kingdom. God allowed an evil spirit to torment Saul because He knew Saul would seek David's help.

The Hebrew word for *torment* is *ba'ath* which means "to be frightened, to overtake, to strike with fear, to be afraid, to dread, to be terrified, to be overtaken by a sudden terror. It is the strongest form of intimidation."[4] Mentally apply this definition to Saul. God allowed the spirit of fear to come on him. Few things torment me like fear. The fear of the future almost kept us from adopting our son. I remember tossing and turning night after night wondering if he'd love us and if he'd obey us. What if he left us after we fell in love with him? I also experienced fear when my oldest daughter got her driver's license. What if someone drove her off the road and hurt her? Fear can be disabling.

Think about a time when you were afraid. What caused it? _____

_____

_____

_____

Saul's attendants searched for a remedy for his torment. His servants found a young man who could play the harp, and they assured the terrorized king that David's songs could

Many of your favorite Psalms were first sung by David, his voice cracking as a teenager to the accompaniment of a well-worn, deeply loved harp.

comfort Saul's soul. David used the harp to bring joyful praises to God and relief to the torments of Saul. Many of your favorite Psalms were first sung by David, his voice cracking as a teenager to the accompaniment of a well-worn, deeply loved harp. Surely the sound of its strings called out to many a straying sheep. The words which accompanied it still do.

Look at 1 Samuel 16:18. What is the next piece of information we learn about David after we are told that he played the harp? _____

_____

_____

_____

David was a complex man. He could be both passionate and withdrawn; dependable and shocking; righteous and wicked—just like us.

In two simple descriptions, God tells us volumes about a man after His own heart. We are shown that David had the tenderness and the sensitivity of an artist. He was a musician and a songwriter. David did not simply have talent. Talent alone could not have soothed the torment of Saul. David plucked the strings of his harp with tenderness and sensitivity. He chose melodies that ministered to the aching soul. Yet, we are also told he was a warrior, brave and strong. The fingers that gently plucked the strings of a harp could wind fiercely around a sling or a sword. We will see his gentle song turn into a public rebuke as he faces the Philistines.

These complementary parts of David's character, recorded in 1 Samuel 16:18, will appear throughout our study. David was a complex man. He could be both passionate and withdrawn; dependable and shocking; righteous and wicked—just like us.

Meditation

Perhaps God brought someone to mind who has been an example to you in both tenderness and strength. Take a moment to think about a mature Christian you know who possesses both these characteristics.

We make a big mistake when we consider being gentle and being a man opposite things. My brother who has such a gift to play the piano could also put a basketball through a hoop, but he was told in junior high he had to make a choice between the two. He was forced to choose either band or sports. He went with his greater gift at the cost of being labeled effeminate.

Two qualities I've come to admire most in both guys and girls are tenderness and strength. I no longer see them as opposite terms. I've come to realize that one without the other leaves an individual incomplete. I deeply desire to be a woman of tenderness and strength because my dearest role model possessed both. Real men can risk being seen as gentle. (And guys, girls love gentlemen!)

Christ Jesus is the artist. He created the world with colors and textures human artists have tried for thousands of years to imitate. Christ Jesus is the musician. He gave the angels their voices. Christ Jesus is the tenderhearted, ministering to our every need.

Christ Jesus is also the warrior, forever leading us in triumphant procession, if only we will follow (2 Cor. 2:14). In our greatest weakness, He is strong. Christ Jesus is the ideal example of both characteristics. He has set an example before us of true manhood and true womanhood. No greater person exists than one who is both tender and strong. David was such a man.

I had the privilege of growing up in Sunday School. I could sit in one of those little wooden chairs in a Sunday School room by the time I could stand. I held my mother's skirt as she walked me to my class as smiling, patient teachers greeted me. I remember the lessons they taught and the pictures they held up to illustrate the stories. It never occurred to me how much easier it would have been for them simply to attend church rather than teach. I'm sure I never said thank you. I should have. Through the stories they told to a bunch of squirming preschoolers, a scary ghost became the living God to me.

We now turn our attention to an account in Scripture that has captured the imaginations of every little boy and girl who ever sat in a circle of small wooden chairs in a Sunday School room. Yes, teacher, some of us were listening. This is the story of David and Goliath. Let's read it again with joy as if for the very first time.

Read 1 Samuel 17:1-58. In your mind, dress Goliath for battle. Picture the pieces of armor described in verses 5-7.

Why did Jesse send David to the camp where his three older brothers were?
❑ to take food to his brothers
❑ to fight against the Philistines with his brothers
❑ to take food to the commander of their unit
❑ to bring back assurance of his sons' well-being

What was promised to the man who killed Goliath?
❑ He would be heir to Saul's throne.
❑ He would receive great wealth.
❑ He would receive Saul's daughter in marriage.
❑ His father's family would be exempt from taxes.

Describe Eliab's feelings toward his youngest brother. _____
_____
_____

Write David's claim to Saul in verse 37. _____
_____
_____
_____

Why didn't David wear Saul's armor? _____
_____
_____
_____

Scripture

" 'The Lord who delivered me from the paw of the lion and the paw of the bear will deliver me from the hand of this Philistine' " (1 Sam. 17:37).

Discovery

You will discover that our victory rests not on faith in our spirituality. Our victory rests on faith in our God.

David still had to face his giant obstacle and use the strength he possessed, but his confidence in God caused a simple pebble to hit like a boulder.

David's greatest weapon actually was not his sling. Read verse 45 carefully. What was David's most powerful weapon? _____

_____

We have already discovered that David possessed qualities of tenderness and strength. We emphasized the quality of tenderness as seen in the soothing way he played the harp. In his confrontation with Goliath we witness the strength of David as a warrior. David had an outlook on the battle that caused God to bring him victory against all odds. David's example teaches us the following guidelines to victory.

1. Take God's Word over the opinions of others. Eliab said everything he possibly could to discourage David. He said David didn't belong, made fun of David's trade, and accused him of having a big head and improper motivation for being at the battle scene. David's response, "Now what have I done?" evidenced the fact that Eliab and David were not at odds for the first time. We see David, not only as the warrior, but as the annoying little brother. I can almost picture him running up behind his brothers, throwing his hands over their eyes, and saying, "Guess who?" They apparently weren't pleased to see him. He could have kept his bread and stayed home for all they cared. I wonder if Eliab's response resulted from almost being anointed king. The first drop of oil had almost fallen on his head when God stopped Samuel and chided him for looking on the outward appearance. For whatever reason, Eliab was very critical of David.

I'm not sure anyone can encourage or discourage us like family. The views of our family members toward us are pretty convincing, aren't they? If the people who know us best encourage us the least, we have few chances to develop confidence.

David remained unshaken by Eliab's criticisms for one reason: David took God's Word over the opinions of others. As Hebrew lads, David and his brothers heard the promises of victory God made to the nation that would call upon His name. David believed those promises. A verse that I've taught my children to memorize that David himself wrote is Psalm 71:5.

Can you remember a time when a family member deeply discouraged you?
❏ Yes ❏ No

God's Word tells us we are loved, gifted, and blessed. We can do anything God calls us to do through Christ who strengthens us (Phil. 4:13). We must develop more confidence in God's Word than in the opinions of others.

David took God's Word over the opinions of others, but that's not all. Let's look at a second guideline to victory from the example of his life.

2. Measure the size of your obstacle against the size of your God. David wanted God to use him to bring Israel victory in the name of the Lord. He had just one obstacle: Goliath. Goliath was over 9 feet tall with over 140 pounds of armor shielding him.

We tend to measure our obstacles against our own strength. We often feel overwhelmed and defeated before the battle even begins. For example, drinking can be one such obstacle. Others may warn of the risk of loss of control, poor judgment, and even alcoholism. A guy may be convinced that God's will is for him to be healthy. The victory would be good health. But the obstacle is a giant—an addiction that seems much stronger than he is. He is discouraged because he is measuring his obstacle against the size of his strength rather than the size of his God. I am not suggesting that if we measure our obstacles against God, our battles will be effortless. David still had to face his giant obstacle and use the strength he possessed, but his confidence in God caused a simple pebble to hit like a boulder.

Is there an area in your life in which God wants to give you a victory but an obstacle seems too big to overcome? ❏ Yes ❏ No

What obstacle must you overcome?_____
_____
_____

3. Acknowledge an active and living God in your life. The description David often used of his Commander-in-Chief demonstrates another basis for his courage.

How did David refer to God in 1 Samuel 17:26?_____
_____

Our victory rests on faith in our God. We're often intimidated in battle because we are uncertain of our faith. We must remember we don't stand in victory because of our faith. We stand in victory because of our God. Faith in faith is pointless. Faith in a living, active God moves mountains. Moses acknowledged Jehovah as the living God and led multitudes to freedom from slavery. Joshua acknowledged Jehovah as the living God and led multitudes into the promised land. Daniel acknowledged Jehovah as the living God and the angel shut the mouths of lions. You serve the same God. Are you allowing Him to live smack in the middle of your life? If so, I bet you've crossed a few Red Seas, tumbled down a few walls, and escaped a few lions yourself. He is alive. He is active. He wants to make you living proof. Remember, the cross would have been God's worst defeat had the people not had cause to exclaim, "He's alive!"

Stories don't get any better than David and Goliath, do they? Stories like the one we've studied today caused the preschooler, who once listened from a baby bear chair, to stand in front of momma bear chairs and teach Sunday School. Some stories are worth retelling. A living God is worth believing.

[1]Spiros Zodhiates, *The Complete Word Study Dictionary: New Testament* (Chattanooga, TN: AMG Publishers, 1992), 1091
[2]Trent C. Butler et al., eds., *Holman Bible Dictionary* (Nashville: Holman Bible Publishers, 1991), 774.
[3]Spiros Zodhiates, *The Complete Word Study Old Testament* (Chattanooga, TN: AMG Publishers, 1994), 2363.
[4]Ibid., 2306.

Faith in faith is pointless. Faith in a living, active God moves mountains.

Ask God to be your confidence when faced with the opinions of others who are stumbling blocks to you.

Chapter Two

FRIENDS AND ENEMIES

Lasting friendships are those which find
their source and strength in God.

Scripture

"Jonathan made a
covenant with David
because he loved him
as himself"
(1 Sam. 18:3).

I n chapter 1, we saw how King Saul's rebellion led to the departure of the Holy
Spirit. David was anointed God's chosen king. Fifteen years passed before he was
crowned. But not one year was wasted. God taught His servant that submission to
Him is the best preparation for an assignment from Him. God allowed David to face
many trials, but He taught David volumes about Himself. Each trial prepared David to
do a work after God's own heart. In this chapter we will witness a tragic turning point in
the relationship between Saul and David, but for now let's take a look at two friends.

Read 1 Samuel 18:1-4. Below describe Jonathan's feelings for David.

_____

_____

_____

Discovery

You will discover that Jonathan's love and friendship toward David is one of the best examples of covenant in God's Word.

Which of the following statements best describes David's feelings for Jonathan according to 1 Samuel 18:1-4?
❑ David loved Jonathan as himself.
❑ David was overwhelmed by the covenant with Jonathan.
❑ David regarded Jonathan as his best friend.
❑ David's feelings toward Jonathan are not mentioned in the covenant.

What did Jonathan give to David in the covenant?
❑ bow ❑ turban ❑ tunic ❑ robe ❑ sword ❑ belt ❑ shield

Sometimes friendships develop over months or years. Other times someone touches your heart almost instantly, and you seem to have known him or her forever.

Have you ever felt an almost instant bond to a new friend? Why do you believe you felt such a bond? _____

_____

_____

Jonathan's expressions of love and friendship toward David are one of the best examples of covenant in the Word of God. The word *covenant* in 1 Samuel 18:3 is derived from the Hebrew term, *berith*, which means, "determination, stipulation, covenant. It was a treaty, alliance of friendship, a pledge, an obligation between a monarch and his subjects, a constitution. It was a contract which was accompanied by signs, sacrifices and a solemn oath which sealed the relationship with promises of blessing for obedience and curses for disobedience."[1]

According to the preceding definition, what three elements accompanied the making of a covenant?
1. _____ 2. _____ 3. _____

Although they are less obvious than in other covenants in Scripture, each of the three elements of covenant can be found in the covenant relationship between Jonathan and David recorded in 1 Samuel 18:1-4. We will look at a covenant in which the elements are more obvious. It will help us understand what we're looking for in Jonathan and David's covenant.

Read Genesis 15. Look for the sign of the covenant, the sacrifice of the covenant, and the solemn oath of the covenant. Briefly describe each element in God's covenant with Abram.
1. Sign (how the covenant was demonstrated): _____

_____

25

2. Sacrifice: _____
_____

3. Solemn oath: _____
_____

You may have identified the sign of the covenant as the smoking firepot with a blazing torch passing between the pieces of flesh. The sacrifice was the heifer, goat, ram, dove, and young pigeon. The solemn oath was the promise to give Abram and his descendants the land. Compare Jonathan's covenant with David by noting the same three elements. Reread 1 Samuel 18:1-4, looking for hints of the three elements of covenant. They are less obvious than the elements in God's covenant with Abram. The sign will likely be the only obvious element. We will discover the other two together.

The sign: Which of the following was the demonstration of the covenant Jonathan made with David?
❏ **Jonathan loved David as himself.**
❏ **David never returned to his father's house.**
❏ **Jonathan gave David his robe, tunic, and weapons.**

God demonstrated His covenant with Abram by the blazing firepot passing between the pieces of flesh. Jonathan demonstrated his covenant with David by giving him his robe, tunic, and weapons. We will see the greater significance of Jonathan's demonstration as we consider the sacrifice and the solemn oath.

The sacrifice: In Jonathan's covenant with David the sacrifice is less obvious than the birds and animals in God's covenant with Abram, but it is profound. Read 1 Samuel 20:30-31. What were King Saul's obvious intentions for his son Jonathan?

_____
_____

Jonathan was a prince and heir apparent to the throne. His father obviously planned for Jonathan to be the next king of Israel, but his son had other plans. In David, Jonathan saw character fit for a king. He was so determined that the throne be occupied by God's chosen instrument he offered everything he had. In this unique covenant, Jonathan sacrificed himself. Jonathan removed his royal clothes—his robe and tunic—and placed it on David, symbolizing that David would be king instead of him. Can you picture David's face as he wears his new clothes while still smelling like sheep?

Jonathan acknowledged David as prince of the Hebrew nation, a position which he could have jealously and eagerly claimed as his own. Men like Jonathan are rare. Few people have "in mind the things of God" at the risk of their own favor and position (Matt. 16:23).

Do you know someone like Jonathan? Do you know anyone who has given up power or position for God's will? ❏ **Yes** ❏ **No**

The solemn oath: Compare 1 Samuel 18:4 and 20:13. How did Jonathan's actions in the first Scripture portray what he said in the second passage?_____

_____

_____

Few people have "in mind the things of God" at the risk of their own favor and position.

The oath of Jonathan's covenant with David does not take place in words in chapter 18. It is symbolized in 1 Samuel 18:4; then it is verbalized in 1 Samuel 20:13. Jonathan symbolized the solemn oath by giving David his weapons of protection: his sword, bow, and belt. He symbolically gave all he had to protect David from harm and ensure his position as future king. Jonathan verbalized his solemn oath by pledging in 1 Samuel 20:13 to protect David from harm at great personal risk.

We have compared two examples of covenant, but we have not yet noted the most meaningful common denominator they share: the basis of the covenant.

According to Deuteronomy 7:6-9, why did God choose the nation of Israel?
❏ **They were the fewest of all peoples.**
❏ **God loved them.**
❏ **They had honored God with their sacrifices.**
❏ **They loved God.**

Look again at Jonathan's covenant with David. What was the basis of their covenant? _____

_____

_____

_____

_____

Does 1 Samuel 18:1-4 mention David returning the love? ❏ **Yes** ❏ **No**

God's covenant with the nation of Israel was based on His love for them. In this same way, Jonathan's covenant with David was based on Jonathan's love, not David's response. We who have accepted Christ as Savior are part of the most wonderful covenant God ever made with man. God loves us for one reason—He chooses to love us.

According to 1 John 4:10,15 how does our covenant compare to the two we've studied? _____

_____

_____

God loves us for one reason—He chooses to love us.

- The sign—God sent His only Son.
- The sacrifice—He "sent his Son as an atoning sacrifice for our sins" (v. 10).
- The solemn oath—"If anyone acknowledges that Jesus is the Son of God, God lives in him and he in God" (v. 15).

Meditation

When and how did you accept Christ as Savior?

My Commitment

_____
_____
_____
_____
_____
_____
_____
_____
_____
_____
_____
_____
_____
_____
_____
_____
_____
_____
_____
_____
_____
_____
_____
_____

The basis of this covenant is the same as the basis of Jonathan's covenant with David–"Not that we loved God but that he loved us" (v. 10). What greater covenant could possibly exist?

We have discovered that covenant is a very important theme in the Word of God. God's covenant with Abram made Jonathan's covenant with David a little clearer. I pray that our look at both covenants makes God's covenant with us dearer.

If you are unsure that you have entered into the covenant of eternal life through the death of Christ, would you consider accepting Christ as Savior right now? The steps to eternal life are simple, but the results are awesome and everlasting:
• Tell God that you are a sinner and you cannot earn eternal life.
• Tell God that you believe Jesus Christ is the Son of God and He died on the cross for you.
• Ask Jesus to forgive you of your sins and to live in your heart through His Holy Spirit.
• Commit your life to love and serve Him.
• Thank God for your new salvation.

If you have accepted Christ as Savior, would you write your commitment in the margin and share your decision with a trusted Christian friend? If you are already a Christian, take time to pray. Thank God for His salvation. Pray for someone you know who has never accepted Christ as Savior.

John Dryden, a sixteenth century philosopher who you may have already encountered in an English class, once called it "the jaundice of the soul."[2] The Song of Solomon says it is as "cruel as the grave" (Song of Sol. 8:6, KJV). Others call it the green-eyed monster. It sends some to jail; others to insanity. It is *jealousy*.

In contrast to Jonathan's self-sacrifice and solemn allegiance, Saul regarded David as the ultimate threat. We will see a seed of jealousy planted deep within the soul of Saul. That seed will show up with a vengeance over many chapters to come. The Scripture we read will expose the evil in the heart of Saul.

Read 1 Samuel 18:5-16. How did David perform the duties Saul assigned to him?
❑ He performed all his duties successfully.
❑ He did what was right in his own eyes.
❑ He was reluctant to obey the commands of Saul.

What did Saul do as a result of David's performance?
❑ He made David his armor-bearer.
❑ He made David second in command.
❑ He gave David a high rank in the army.

What first ignited the jealousy of King Saul? (v. 7) _____
_____

How did Saul's inward jealousy become an outward violent expression? _____
_____
_____

According to verse 14 why was David a great success in everything he did? _____
_____
_____

We have identified several feelings Saul had toward David. Read the list of feelings below and cross out any which do not describe Saul's feelings as mentioned in 1 Samuel 18:5-16.

admiration	jealousy	hatred	fear	joy
gall	anger	anticipation	anxiety	

I believe that *fear* is the root of virtually all jealousy. Consider the possible relationship between fear and jealousy by responding to the following scenarios.

Why might a girl be jealous of her boyfriend working as a lab partner with another girl? _____
_____
_____

Why might a guy be jealous of a new, talented athlete playing a similar position to his own? _____
_____
_____

Do you see how fear might contribute to both cases of jealousy? We could discuss countless examples of jealousy fueled by fear, but we don't need to look further than 1 Samuel 18. Saul was terribly jealous of David.

What fear might have fueled the jealousy? _____
_____
_____

Just as fear often leads to jealousy, most negative emotions lead to others. I see at least four emotions attributed to Saul in his reactions to David. In verse 8 we see anger and gall, which ordinarily means bitterness. In verse 9 we see jealousy, and in verses 12 and 15 we see evidences of fear. When emotions are unchecked by the Holy Spirit, one negative emotion can easily feed another, joining together as links in a chain that keeps us captive. Knowing the original Hebrew word for the kind of anger Saul experienced is helpful:

Scripture

"They have credited David with tens of thousands," he [Saul] thought, "but me with only thousands. What more can he get but the kingdom?" And from that time on Saul kept a jealous eye on David (1 Sam. 18:8-9).

Fear is the root of virtually all jealousy.

When emotions are unchecked by the Holy Spirit, one negative emotion can easily feed another.

Discovery

You will discover that just as fear often leads to jealousy, most negative emotions result in destructive consequences.

Anger: *Charah*—to burn, be kindled, glow with anger, be incensed, grow indignant; to be zealous, act zealously. Unlike some of its synonyms, *charah* points to the fire or heat of the anger just after it has been ignited.[3]

Charah captures the moment a person explodes with anger—the moment anger is ignited before any sense of control takes over, before a rational thought can be processed.

When was the last time you exploded over something? _____
_____
_____

Did you have any regrets later? ❑ Yes ❑ No **If so, describe them below.** _____
_____
_____
_____

Rarely do we accomplish anything profitable at the moment we become angry. Actions or words immediately following the ignition of anger are almost always regrettable. Moments like the one *charah* describes are exactly the reason why I never want to approach a day without praying to be filled with the Holy Spirit. Through the life of Saul, we see a portrait of what our lives might be like if the Holy Spirit either departed or was quenched in us. *No thanks!*

Saul felt many things toward David, but the most consistent emotion was jealousy. Two men will pay a tremendous price for the jealousy of Saul. We will witness some of the suffering jealousy showered on the lives of both Saul and David. Few experiences are more miserable than being the subject of someone's unleashed jealousy. Perhaps the only thing worse is being the one in whom the jealousy rages. Let's count the cost of being subject to someone's jealousy; then determine whether or not jealousy is ever a healthy emotion.

In Acts 5:17-18 what happened as a result of jealousy? _____
_____
_____

According to Acts 5:19, who rescued them from the wages of jealousy? _____
_____
_____

Describe the results of jealousy in Acts 13:44-50. _____
_____
_____

In Acts 13:49, what did God do through them in spite of their jealousy? _____
_____
_____

If you are the innocent subject of someone's unchecked jealousy—at school, at church, in a relationship—tell God on him or her! Let God work. Pray for Him to deliver you, to sow peace in your persecutor's heart, and to move powerfully in spite of the wrongful response of another. If you are a sower of jealousy in your own heart, I urge you to ask God right now to release you from its bondage and fill you with His Spirit.

What does 1 Corinthians 3:3 tell you about jealousy?
☐ Jealousy is characteristic of worldly behavior.
☐ Jealousy is evidence that the enemy is at work.
☐ Jealousy is overcome by forgiveness.

Is jealousy ever a proper response? Does it ever sow good rather than evil? Believe it or not, the answer is yes!

What is a righteous kind of jealousy according to 2 Corinthians 11:2? _____
_____
_____
_____
_____
_____

What does Exodus 20:5 tell us about jealousy? _____
_____
_____
_____
_____

What kind of jealousy does God possess? Fill in the missing words.

Joel 2:18:   "The Lord will be jealous _____ his land and take pity on his people."

Zechariah 1:14: "This is what the Lord Almighty says, 'I am very jealous _____ Jerusalem and Zion.' "

Zechariah 8:2:   This is what the Lord Almighty says, "I am very jealous _____ Zion; I am burning with jealousy for her."

2 Corinthians 11:2: "I am jealous _____ you with a godly jealousy."

Do you see a common characteristic in all righteous jealousies? A big difference exists between being jealous *of* someone and being jealous *for* someone. God is jealous on our behalf. He is jealous for us to know the One True God. He is jealous for us to be in a state of blessing. He is jealous for us to be kept from the evil one. He is jealous for us to be ready for our Bridegroom. Jealousy *for* someone's best is of God. Jealousy *of* someone's best is of the enemy.

Jealousy for someone's best is of God. Jealousy of someone's best is of the enemy.

Meditation

Is there anyone you are jealous "for"? Who is it and what is the nature of your righteous jealousy on his or her behalf? Ask God to protect your relationship.

Read 1 Samuel 18:17-30. Why was Saul pleased that his daughter was in love with David? What does his attitude tell you about his heart? _____

_____

_____

_____

Why did Saul become more afraid once he realized his daughter loved David? _____

_____

_____

_____

> **David had something much greater than high hopes. He had a Most High God.**

So David is married. We know little about Michal, but Saul considered the marriage a way to destroy David (v. 21). Can you imagine the evil in the heart of a man who would use his own daughter as a pawn in a personal vendetta against someone else? Perhaps Saul was raised on a well-known story of another man gifted with strength, who struck down a thousand men with the jawbone of a donkey, but could not tame one little woman. Samson went straight from the hands of Delilah into the hands of the Philistines and ultimately to his death (Judg. 15; 16). Saul obviously had high hopes that Michal would be the death of David, but David had something much greater than high hopes. He had a Most High God.

We have seen the seed of jealousy sown in the heart of Saul. Fear, anger, and bitterness fueled a jealousy that quickly grew out of control. We continue to see the power of jealousy contrasted with the power of love and the Spirit. As I first read 1 Samuel 19, I could almost see the scene unfold on stage. Picture the scene with me.

Read 1 Samuel 19:1-18. In what ways did Jonathan respond to his father's orders to kill David?
❑ He warned David of his father's intentions.
❑ He pretended to follow his father's instructions.
❑ He reminded his father how David had benefited him.
❑ He broke his covenant with David to honor his father.

What was the result of Jonathan's efforts in David's behalf?
❑ Saul regarded Jonathan as a traitor.
❑ Saul's anger toward David deepened.
❑ Saul and David were briefly reconciled.
❑ An evil spirit struck Saul.

How did Michal demonstrate her love for David in 1 Samuel 19? _____

_____

_____

Scripture

Jonathan spoke well of David to Saul his father and said to him, "Let not the king do wrong to his servant David; he has not wronged you, and what he has done has benefited you greatly" (1 Sam. 19:4).

In verse 17 what excuse did Michal give her father for deceiving him? _____

_____

_____

Now, that's drama, isn't it? We continue our look at the power of jealousy.

First consider how Saul's jealousy continued to grow. Jonathan was momentarily able to bring his father back to reality. He tried to convince Saul that David had been good for him and for the kingdom. Jonathan reminded Saul that he had initially been glad over David's victory. Keep in mind that Jonathan risked his own life in keeping the covenant with David. Saul did not hesitate to order Jonathan's death once before. If Saul's men had not talked him into being rational, he would have killed his own son. (See 1 Sam. 14:43-45.) Well-chosen words calmed Saul's jealous rage, but it returned with a vengeance. Without God's intervention, we can offer only a small bandage to someone wasting away from uncontrolled emotions. We may bring calm for a moment, but our efforts will have little lasting effect.

Do you remember a time when you talked someone out of negative thoughts and feelings only to see the person become captivated again? ❏ **Yes** ❏ **No**
If so, in the margin briefly describe the events.

Have you ever been talked out of a negative state of mind and emotions only to be captivated by those feelings again? If so, describe the situation. _____

_____

_____

_____

Meditation

Our words can only treat the symptoms. Only God can heal the disease of uncontrolled emotions. We've probably all been in Saul's place at one time or another. Something makes us furious; then someone tries to "talk some sense into us." We feel a little better and pledge to put our anger away forever. Then, here it comes again with the power of gale-force winds. Our emotions negatively ignited can be more powerful than we are. Our best recourse when negative emotions begin controlling us is to fall before the throne of grace and seek God! Take comfort in the fact that Christ knows how it feels to be tempted by feelings (Heb. 2:18; 4:15).

Saul failed to acknowledge his rage and jealousy as evil. His imagination did nothing but further sow the seed within him, and his jealousy became unmerciful. Our imaginations will also fuel the fires of jealousy if we are not careful.

Jealousy is a powerful emotion, but so is love. Look back at 1 Samuel 18:28-29. Why was Saul frightened when he realized that Michal loved David? _____

_____

_____

_____

Think about a time when you have struggled with overcoming your anger. How did God use His Spirit, other people, and divine circumstances to carry you through it.

Discovery

You will discover that love is more powerful than jealousy, godliness is more powerful than wickedness, and the Spirit of God is more powerful than anything!

When God gets involved, we see real results.

Saul was right about love threatening his plans for Michal to bring harm to David. The power of love often exceeds the power of loyalty. He thought he could trust Michal to make David miserable. He thought she would be a puppet in his hands against the young warrior until he realized she loved him. Her masterful deception could easily have led to her death. Surely she was only spared because she convinced her father that David would have killed her if she hadn't let him get away.

A vital piece of information is recorded in verse 18. To whom did David run?
❏ Jonathan ❏ Jesse ❏ Samuel ❏ Eliab

Why did he run to this particular person? _____
_____
_____

Have you ever had a time in your life when someone encouraged you to do something and once you got in the middle of it, you went back and said, "What have you gotten me into?" Have you ever felt that way about a blind date? Auditioning for a play? Trying out for a team? Sharing your testimony in a group setting? David probably shared your doubts and questions. David went straight to Samuel because he was the one God used to anoint David as God's chosen leader of Israel. He likely had questions for Samuel, such as "Are you sure God told you to anoint me?" Regardless of his questions, David went to tell on Saul! Samuel received David and no doubt confirmed his calling.

We've seen proof that love can be more powerful than jealousy. We will also see that the Spirit of God is more powerful than jealousy.

Read 1 Samuel 19:19-24.

These events are almost humorous, aren't they? Saul sent one man after another to capture David, but every time they entered the presence of Samuel's prophets, the Spirit of God fell on them and they prophesied, too! Finally, Saul apparently thought, *Fine. I'll do it myself.* The same thing happened to him!

What do these words in the NIV mean: "The Spirit of God came even upon him"? _
_____
_____
_____

When God gets involved, we see real results. Don't miss celebrating that when a group of evil men met a group of godly men, godliness won. How encouraging to remember that the Spirit of God is more powerful than the spirit of wickedness! As 1 John 4:4 reminds us, "You, dear children, are from God and have overcome them, because the one who is in you is greater than the one who is in the world."

We've seen that love is more powerful than jealousy, godliness is more powerful than wickedness, and the Spirit of God is more powerful than *anything!* The best laid plans of kings and queens crumble under the mighty Spirit of God. Acts 1:8 tells us that when the Holy Spirit comes on us we will receive *power*. The original Greek word is *dunamis*. We call it *dynamite*. That's what it takes to burst the walls of rage and jealousy within us. First John 3:20 states, "God is greater than our hearts."

As children of God, we do not have to be derailed by the way we feel. Our God is greater. Give Him your heart!

First Samuel 20 describes a comparatively simple scene. As we find David caught in the whirlwind of Saul's jealousy, we also see this threat of death give way to the reaffirmation of Jonathan's covenant. We are going to talk about friendships, the "once-in-a-lifetime" kind. Observe the relationship between Jonathan and David and the events that caused their separation.

Read 1 Samuel 20:1-42. Why did David flee to Jonathan? _____
_____

Mark each of the following statements as true or false based on 1 Samuel 20:1-24. If the statement is false, draw a line through the error and correct the statement in the margin.
____ **Jonathan believed that his father was going to kill David.**
____ **Jonathan was to tell Saul that David went to his hometown because of an annual celebration.**
____ **Jonathan pledged to let David know if his father planned to harm him.**
____ **Jonathan would cast his spear by the stone Ezel to let David know Saul's response.**

Jonathan signaled his father's unfavorable response to David just as he promised. Describe the scene between Jonathan and David after the boy had gathered the arrows and departed. _____
_____
_____

Offer a few reasons why you believe David might have "wept the most." _____
_____
_____

We've read about tragic events, but we've seen priceless expressions of deep friendship. In 1 Samuel 18:1-4 we saw the making of the covenant between Jonathan and David. Now we see the keeping of that covenant. Anyone can make a covenant, but only the faithful keep their covenants.

Scripture

" 'Show me unfailing kindness like that of the Lord as long as I live, so that I may not be killed, and do not ever cut off your kindness from my family— not even when the Lord has cut off every one of David's enemies from the face of the earth' " (1 Sam. 20:14-15).

Anyone can make a covenant, but only the faithful keep their covenants.

First Samuel 20 pictures words so beautifully expressed in 1 Samuel 18:1. The Word of God tells us, "Jonathan became one in spirit with David, and he loved him as himself" (1 Sam. 18:1). The *King James Version* helps us draw a more vivid mental image: "the soul of Jonathan was knit with the soul of David." The original Hebrew word translated "knit" in the *King James Version* and "became one" in the *New International Version* is *qashar* which means "to tie … join together, knit."[4] Jonathan and David are examples of two people knit together by something more powerful than circumstances or preferences.

The Spirit of God sometimes cements two people together as part of His plan. God would never have chosen David to be His future king if He had not planned to sustain him, and ultimately deliver him safely to his throne. Jonathan was an important part of God's plan. They were uncommon friends joined by a common bond: the Spirit of God. First Samuel 18:1 tells us that Jonathan and David were united, but 1 Samuel 20 shows us!

Characteristics of Uncommon Friendship

Uncommon friends can speak their minds without fear. Reread 1 Samuel 20:1-4 and imagine the tone David probably used with Jonathan. His words suggest panic. Jonathan could easily have received David's words as an insult. After all, David practically took his frustration out on Jonathan and asked him to explain his father's actions. As you carefully consider the words they traded, you can almost hear their elevated and emotional tones. Jonathan responded to David's panic with the words, "Look, my father doesn't do anything, great or small, without confiding in me. Why would he hide this from me? It's not so!" (See v. 2.) I believe they exchanged heated words. David came very close to holding Jonathan responsible for Saul's actions, and Jonathan came very close to getting defensive.

Their initial words to one another would be only natural under their circumstances. What is not natural, however, was their freedom to speak their minds to one another and move on to resolution without great incident. Notice that at this point Jonathan didn't believe that Saul was really trying to take David's life; yet he acknowledged that David's feelings were authentic by saying, "Whatever you want me to do, I'll do for you" (v. 4). He didn't necessarily agree with David, but he agreed that David was upset and needed his help instead of his doubt.

Each of us can probably remember times when people have focused their frustrations on us and held us responsible for something beyond our control. How do you usually respond to this kind of scenario.
❑ **I ordinarily become a little defensive.**
❑ **I ordinarily become very defensive.**
❑ **I ordinarily allow the person to safely blow some steam.**
❑ **I ordinarily refuse to talk to him or her until he or she settles down.**

The bonds of uncommon friends are deeper than the width of their differences.

Allowing others to speak their fears even when we can't understand is characteristic of uncommon friendship. Willingness to listen, then let the potential insults pass is not a sign of weakness. It is a sign of strength. The bonds of uncommon friends are deeper than the width of their differences.

Can you think of a time when a friend "let you off the hook" when you centered your frustration on him or her? ❑ Yes ❑ No **If yes, briefly explain here:** _____
_____
_____

You will discover the key to true friendship.

Uncommon friends can share their hearts without shame. The scene between Jonathan and David in 1 Samuel 20:41 touches my heart every time I read it. Something about two men unafraid to share their hearts with one another never fails to move me. Uncommon friends can be vulnerable with one another and still retain their dignity. The friendship between Jonathan and David was far more than emotion, and it was a safe place to trust and show feelings. They shared a common goal: the will of God. Each life complemented the other. They had separate lives but inseparable bonds.

My husband Keith runs his family's plumbing business. His best friend Roger is a lawyer and judge. They are uncommon friends. They don't talk every day. They don't necessarily talk every week, but their bonds remain firm. They play jokes on one another. They take up for one another. Roger often sends Keith cards or cartoons. Keith drops by Roger's office unexpectedly with lunch from time to time. When they see one another, they hug. When they hurt, they sometimes cry. They are "real men" with a rare friendship.

Do you sometimes struggle with the appropriate response when someone is very emotional with you? ❑ Yes ❑ No

Read Romans 12:15. Based on this verse, what do you believe people really need from us when they are extremely emotional? _____
_____
_____

Do you have a friend with whom you feel safe sharing your heart? ❑ Yes ❑ No **If your answer is no, and you wish you had an uncommon friend, use the space below to express a prayer for one.** _____
_____
_____
_____

Uncommon friends can stay close even at a distance. Most friendships require time and attention. Jonathan and David's friendship did not grow out of a lengthy period of time as most friendships do. They were brought together by spiritual ties, not sequences of time. They had "sworn friendship with each other in the name of the Lord" (v. 42). God brought them together. Their friendship was a bond of three.

Read Ecclesiastes 4:9-12. This Scripture applies perfectly to Jonathan and David, but give special attention to the last statement in verse 12. How could you apply this statement to God's part in Jonathan and David's friendship? _____
_____
_____

Meditation

Do you have a "three strand" friendship? Is God an active part of one of your friendships? Reflect on the ways you and your friend keep God an active part of your friendship.

I have known the joy of several uncommon friends in my life. God has definitely tied my spirit to the spirits of several wonderful people who have influenced my life and allowed me to share my heart with them. My husband is one such friend. We just can't seem to keep from falling back in love with one another after difficult times. God has also blessed my life with another soul mate. She is more than a friend. She is a partner in the gospel, brought to me by God to be another part of this ministry. We have an unexplainable yoke in our spirits which God ordained for His purposes. We are equally dedicated to one specific goal: to share the Word of God. She does her part. I do mine. God braids the strands with His purpose and forms "a cord of three strands" which is not easily broken.

A very significant season of David's life begins in the next chapter we will study. David was scarcely 20 years old when he was forced to leave his home, his livelihood, and his beloved friend as he fled from the madman who happened to be king of Israel (and the father of his best friend!).

As a college student I suffered enough trauma just leaving home to go to college where I had a secure room in the dorm, a guaranteed meal in the cafeteria, and more company than I could stand. I certainly have nothing with which to compare this season of David's young life. He is on the run with a madman on his heels. Saul had alerted half the country to take David's life. David faced a terrifying prospect for a person twice his age. We now look at David's initiation to life on the run.

Read 1 Samuel 21:1-9. When David resigned to live as a fugitive, he first went to Nob, to Ahimelech the priest. Why do you think Ahimelech might have been frightened by David's coming?_____
_____
_____
_____

What lie did David tell Ahimelech?_____
_____
_____

What two things did David request from the priest?
❑ five loaves of bread   ❑ protection   ❑ prayer   ❑ a weapon

The priest had no bread to offer David except the bread of _____.

Doeg the Edomite will become a memorable figure in the future. Who was he according to verse 7?
❑ One of the priests of Nob   ❑ Ahimelech's head shepherd
❑ One of David's men   ❑ Saul's head shepherd

The only sword in Nob was the one which had belonged to _____.

David did not haphazardly end up in Nob. David no doubt sought relief in the "city of priests." Nob, a village between Jerusalem and Gibeah, was the place where the tabernacle was relocated after the destruction of Shiloh. Like many of us in times of crisis, he may have desired to draw closest to those who seem closest to God–not a bad idea.

When was the last time you reached out to your youth leader, Sunday School teacher, or someone you regard as being "close to God"? Why did you reach out to that particular person in your time of need?_____

_____

_____

_____

In the first verse of chapter 21, we see that Ahimelech "trembled" when he met David. Ahimelech was probably not aware of the warrant out for David's life. If he had known Saul was seeking to kill David, he would not have asked why David was alone. Perhaps verse 9 provides a little insight. Ahimelech knew of Goliath's demise at the hands of this young man. He also may have remembered David sporting through Jerusalem swinging Goliath's head in his hand. No doubt, David was rather intimidating. The priests certainly would have wanted no trouble from the Philistine army seeking revenge. Whatever the reasons, we are told that the sight of David struck fear in the priest's heart.

David responded to the priest with a lie. Through our study we will be witness to more than a few compromises in David's character. In this case the compromise was David's willingness to lie. He was probably attempting to spare the priests' life, hoping that Saul would not hold Ahimelech responsible for helping David.

Famished from his flight, David asked the priest for bread. He asked for five loaves.

Christ fed the multitudes with _____ loaves of bread in Matthew 14:19.

Interestingly, David requested in verse 3, "Give me five loaves of bread, or whatever you can find." In all four of the Gospels, as Christ sent the disciples to search for food, five loaves were all they could find. For David, however, no bread could be found except the bread of the Presence. Perhaps God had a point to make with the five loaves. Let's do a little research about the bread of the Presence.

Read Leviticus 24:5-9. Fill in the following blank. Verse 8 says, "This bread is to be set out before the Lord regularly, Sabbath after Sabbath, on behalf of the Israelites, as _____."

Now read Isaiah 55:3. What was God's "everlasting covenant" in this verse?
❑ never cut off His people from their inheritance
❑ restore the promised land to the people of Israel
❑ promised His faithful love to David
❑ promised His faithful love to Abraham

Scripture

"The priest gave him the consecrated bread, since there was no bread there except the bread of the Presence that had been removed from before the Lord and replaced by hot bread on the day it was taken away" (1 Sam. 21:6).

Discovery

You will discover that God is true to His word. Through the Sprit of Christ, God is always with us.

God also extends His presence to you as your sustaining provision.

Consider two possible reasons why the bread of the Presence might have purposely been used of God to feed David:

1. The bread of the Presence might have symbolized God's everlasting covenant with David. Somewhat like the stars of the sky symbolized the offspring of Abram (Gen. 15:5), the bread of the Presence was placed before God as a reminder, or symbol, of the everlasting covenant. Through the bread of the Presence God may have been "reminding" David that He had not broken the everlasting covenant He had made with David's kingdom.

2. The bread of the Presence might have symbolized the provision of God's presence in the life of David. Just as the first possible reason was a corporate symbol for a kingdom covenant, I believe the second reason might have been a private symbol for a personal covenant. The original Hebrew term for *presence* is *paneh* which means, "countenance, presence, or face."[4] The everlasting covenant symbolized by the bread of the Presence was a reminder of the pledge of God's presence to His people. As He offered bread to David through Ahimelech the priest, I believe God pledged His presence to David throughout his exile. God inspired David to write the two verses below.

Look up each of the following verses and fill in the missing words:

Psalm 22:24, "He has not despised or disdained the suffering of the afflicted one; he has not _____ from him but has listened to his cry for help."

Psalm 31:16, "Let your _____, save me in your unfailing love."

The original word for *face* in both the above verses is *paneh*, the exact original word for *presence* in the phrase "the bread of the Presence." God was doing more in this moment in Nob than feeding David's hungry stomach. I believe He was pledging His presence to him and promising to be his complete sustainer. God also extends His presence to you as your sustaining provision.

Read John 6:47-48. By what name does Christ call Himself? _____

What hint do you see of "covenant" (something binding or perpetual) in John 6:47?

_____
_____
_____

Christ is the bread of God's presence to us.

Christ is the bread of God's presence to us. His scars are placed before God as a perpetual memorial that the wages of our sins have been paid. Christ said, "This bread is my flesh, which I will give for the life of the world" (John 6:51). Those who have eaten the bread of His Presence enjoy the same everlasting covenant He made with David thousands of years ago. He renews His promise to us in Hebrews 13:5: "Never will I leave you; never will I forsake you."

You have probably gone through difficulties in which you felt lost and afraid. Can you think of ways God has reminded you that He was with you, that His "presence" was there? _____

_____

God reminded David of His presence but David continued to run frantically from village to village. Surely Samuel reminded David of God's plan when David fled to Ramah. God reminded David of His presence and provision through the priest of Nob. God reminded David in another way. Is it coincidental that the only weapon in the city of Nob was Goliath's? Is it possible God was trying to remind David that he had overcome a greater enemy than Saul with God's help? None of these reminders seemed to help, because David had forgotten to measure his obstacle against his God rather than against his own strength (as he had Goliath)! At least his relentless search for refuge led to a rather humorous scene which we now view briefly.

Read 1 Samuel 21:10-15. Had David been auditioning for a theatrical production, he would no doubt have gotten the part! Describe David's "act" in the lines below. __
_____

_____

Why did David put on this "act"?_____
_____

_____

Not only was David a harpist and a warrior, he could have won an Oscar for best actor! Some people act for pleasure. Others act for money. David was acting for his life. He pulled it off, too. You may be wondering why the men of Gath didn't kill him on the spot. They were terrified of a madman and far too superstitious to harm one. They feared he was a dangerous demon who had the power to cause them havoc from the next life. Apparently, David wasn't just sheep smart, he was street smart. To David's good fortune, Achish had enough madmen to deal with and had no desire to have one "carrying on" in front of him.

David may have been short on patience and short on perceiving God's constant reminders, but David certainly wasn't short on personality, was he? Patience and perception might have helped him a little more than personality.

In the next chapter we will join David as he negotiates some pretty tough times. We'll begin to peek a little deeper into the heart God saw and loved. Studying God's Word is habit forming. Keep praying for a hunger and thirst for His Word. Like David, God doesn't want you feeding from common loaves. He desires to feed you with the bread of His Presence. His table is always set.

David had forgotten to measure his obstacle against his God rather than against his own strength.

Ask God to make you aware of the constant reminders of His presence in your life so that you can have His assurance no matter your circumstances.

[1] Spiros Zodhiates, *The Complete Word Study Old Testament* (Chattanooga, TN: AMG Publishers, 1994), 2306.
[2] John Dryden, "The Hind and the Panther," *The Poetical Works of John Dryden*, Cambridge Edition, ed. George R. Noyes (Boston: Houghton Mifflin Company, 1909), 236.
[3] *The Complete Word Study Old Testament*, 2318.
[4] Ibid., 105.

Scripture

I pour out my complaint before him; before him I tell my trouble. When my spirit grows faint within me, it is you who know my way. In the path where I walk men have hidden a snare for me (Ps. 142:2-3).

Chapter Three

ALONE WITH GOD

No matter how desperate the circumstances God never leaves His children.

L et's take some time to consider an important part of David's experience that provided painful preparation for the throne God had promised. Filled with dreams and wonderful expectations, our young hero David was met by a nightmare. He had not only left his home, now he ran from his "home away from home." He was separated from his new wife and his best friend, and forced to beg for food from the priest of Nob.

Read 1 Samuel 22:1-5.

According to these verses where was David and who visited him? _____
_____

Let's look at the Psalm that David wrote after he went to the cave.

Read Psalm 142. Based on the example David provides in Psalm 142, read the
following statements about prayer and mark each one true or false.
_____ I should not pray for myself but only for the needs of others.
_____ Bringing my complaint to God is inappropriate.
_____ God cares how I feel.
_____ Asking to be rescued from danger is unspiritual.

In one sentence state the theme of Psalm 142. _____
_____
_____

Few of us have been forced to hide in a cave in order to be safe, but all of us have felt some of the same emotions David experienced.

Discovery

You will discover that no matter how bad things look, God is good.

Few of us have been forced to hide in a cave in order to be safe, but all of us have felt some of the same emotions David experienced. Psalm 142 offers a number of insights into David's heart. His responses provide an example for us. What did David do when he was overwhelmed with unfair treatment and difficult circumstances?

1. *David prayed.* Be careful not to overlook David's most obvious response. David responded to his difficulty with prayer. We should pray about everything.

2. *David cried aloud.* The scene touches my heart as I imagine this young man sobbing in the cave. Once I was nearby when a teenager slammed his hand in a car door and could not remove it for at least a minute. He was in incredible pain. I watched him as he struggled between his internal need to cry like a baby and his external need to "be cool" and keep his dignity. David too wanted to act like a man, but he was virtually a boy in a situation any adult would consider frightening.

David was a real man by anyone's standards, yet he knew no better way to deal with his situation than crying aloud to his God. "Cry aloud to the Lord" when you feel overwhelmed. He can take it!

3. *David poured out his complaint to God.* Tell God what's hurting you. You can even tell Him what's bugging you! I am convinced this is one of the major truths that contributes to David's Godlike heart.

Write David's words from Psalm 62:8. _____
_____
_____
_____
_____

43

Just because no one is there for us doesn't mean that no one cares.

Meditation

Is there something that you really need to say to God right now? If there is take a few quiet moments and talk to God. If there is nothing specific right now, thank God for His constant protection in your life.

4. David rehearsed his trust in God. In Psalm 142:3, David said, "When my spirit grows faint within me, it is you who know my way." His prayer to God also became a reminder to himself: "God knows my way." Prayer is for our sake as much as it is for God's pleasure.

5. David longed for God's presence. David was alone. He felt that no one cared. Although he had found a cave in which to hide, David felt he had no refuge because no one was there who cared for him. We often equate safety with people, not places. In times of trouble, just because no one is there for us doesn't mean that no one cares.

Have you ever felt like David? When was the last time you felt like no one was there to be a refuge in your time of need? _____
_____
_____

Certainly many people cared for David, but because they were not physically present, he felt abandoned. His feelings did not reflect the truth, but they were worthy to share with God.

6. David confessed his desperate need. In Psalm 142:6 he said, "Listen to my cry, for I am in desperate need; rescue me from those who pursue me, for they are too strong for me." A wise man knows when those who stand against him are mightier than he is! David had killed both a lion and a bear; then Goliath became "like one of them" (1 Sam. 17:36). David knew that God had given him power to defeat all three enemies.

Read 1 Samuel 22:6-23.

Why do you think the king's officials disobeyed Saul's orders? _____
_____
_____
_____

Read Psalm 52.

Assuming David is addressing Saul, in verse 1 what does David accuse Saul of doing? _____
_____
_____
_____

The first verse of this Psalm strongly suggests that Saul not only had a multitude of innocent people put to death–many of them priests–he also bragged about it. In the spring of 1995, our nation experienced terror, violence, and tragedy, only to discover the perpetrators to be some of our own countrymen. For weeks, workers removed the rubble of the Federal Building in Oklahoma City. Imagine how U.S. citizens would have felt if the person responsible began to brag about the crime. We would feel the way David did. That's exactly how Saul behaved.

Have you ever known anyone who made him or herself feel bigger or better by putting others down? ❑ Yes ❑ No **What did you believe those actions said about the person?** _____

_____

_____

_____

_____

Putting others down to build ourselves up is perhaps the ultimate sign of insecurity. If we allow our insecurities to govern our lives, we become destroyers just as certainly as this insane king did.

When was the last time you were stunned by the way a person behaved? _____

_____

_____

_____

_____

I will never forget seeing the first film clips on television from the Oklahoma City bombing. Two years prior to the tragedy, I had been asked to speak at a conference in the Oklahoma City area. The conference would take place the day following the bombing. I kept thinking that perhaps we would cancel the event; or perhaps many would not attend. The event was not cancelled. Only one person who registered did not come. She was unaccounted for in the rubble of the Federal Building. Never in my entire ministry have I been more frightened that I might give the wrong message. I begged God to be clear with me and not let me say a word on my own. My text was different than Psalm 52, yet the points He sent me to make were almost identical to the ones we've noted:
1. God is not the author of destruction.
2. God will repay evil.
3. Our hope must be in God.
4. No matter how bad things look, God is good.

How can each of the following Scriptures help you sort things out when tragedies happen?

John 10:10 _____

_____

_____

_____

_____

Lamentations 3:33 _____

_____

_____

_____

_____

Scripture

I will sacrifice a freewill offering to you; I will praise your name, O Lord, for it is good (Ps. 54:6).

et's take a look at how David sought to escape the demented King Saul. We will learn that David did more than hide. David took every possible opportunity to defend his people, even when he was repaid with betrayal.

Read 1 Samuel 23. What did David do before he defended the people of Keilah?

_____
_____
_____

How did David's men react to his instruction from God?
❑ **They were thrilled.**
❑ **They were afraid.**
❑ **They were angry.**
❑ **Other:** _____

Do you think David was wrong to ask for God's direction a second time? Why or why not? _____
_____
_____
_____
_____
_____

Discovery

You will discover that if you honor a person out of respect for God, God will honor you.

Tucked into the priestly ephod were the sacred lots. An ephod was the upper garment worn by the Jewish priests. Casting the lots was nothing like throwing dice. These lots were ordained by God as a means by which He would guide His people in making decisions that were not specifically addressed in the written Word at that time. You and I have the privilege of "knowing the rest of the story." God's Word is now written in its entirety. We don't need sacred lots. We just need "lots" of study!

David received two answers from God through the ephod. What were they? Choose two.
❑ **Saul would pursue him.**
❑ **Jonathan would provide shelter for him.**
❑ **The citizens of Keilah would give David over to Saul.**
❑ **David would be victorious.**

Why did God send Jonathan to David at this time? _____
_____
_____
_____
_____

Have you ever noticed that God's faithfulness appears brighter when the backdrop of our lives looks bleak and gray? This chapter shows God's faithfulness shining brightly against the gloomy backdrop of David's life. Consider two specific evidences of God's faithfulness to David based on 1 Samuel 23:

1. *God reconfirmed His directions to David.*

When was the last time you "double-checked" God's direction in your life? ____
_____
_____

Did you feel faithless for asking a second time? ❏ Yes ❏ No

David's example reminds us that doubting God and doubting that we understand God are two different things. Look at a second evidence of God's faithfulness to David.

2. *God sent David a minister of encouragement.* Jonathan went to David and "helped him find strength in God" (v. 16). In effect, God sent Jonathan to say, "You can trust Me to fulfill what I promised you, and you can trust Jonathan not to turn his back on you."

When was the last time God sent you a minister of encouragement to help you find strength in God?_____
_____
_____
_____
_____

Read Psalm 54. How did David ask God to save him (v. 1)?
❏ **by His outstretched arm**
❏ **by His goodness**
❏ **by His love**
❏ **other:** _____

In Psalm 54:6 what did David vow he would do?
❏ **sacrifice a freewill offering**
❏ **get revenge on Saul**
❏ **stay faithful forever**
❏ **tell of His salvation**

> **Doubting God and doubting we understand God are two different things.**

David began Psalm 54 with the words, "Save me, O God, by your name." We will see David call on God by a multitude of names. A name meant far more than individual identification to the Hebrew people. A name represented the person's character. David seemed to have as many names for God as he had needs! Why? Because God was everything to him! One of my favorite ways David referred to God is when he uses the little word "my." In Psalm 62:6-7 he said, "He alone is *my* rock and *my* salvation; he is *my* fortress . . . *my* mighty rock, *my* refuge." Aren't you glad his God can be yours and mine as well?

Meditation

When was the last time the conviction of the Holy Spirit struck your conscience and you immediately responded with a change in behavior?

The Holy Spirit always does His job, but we don't always do ours. If we are filled by His Spirit, conviction will result in a change in behavior.

What does David's approach reveal to you about his relationship with God? _____
_____
_____
_____
_____

God often works the same sequence in us that He worked in David:
1. He calls us.
2. He prepares us.
3. He uses us.
4. He prepares us some more.
5. He uses us some more.

Read 1 Samuel 24:6. Why did David believe he should not lift a hand against Saul? _____
_____
_____

What evidence can you find to support the following statement: Although David assured Saul he would not harm him, he did not absolve (pardon) him of wrong-doing? _____
_____
_____

David apparently chose to risk the brunt of man's disapproval over God's disapproval, regardless of the consequences. David's change of heart offers four evidences that He was greatly influenced by the Holy Spirit.

1. David's conscience was immediately stricken. One of the most important jobs of the Holy Spirit is to convict of sin (John 16:8). When the Holy Spirit dwells in a person, He uses the individual's conscience as the place where conviction is experienced.

Can you recall a time when you used the excuse, "Well, at least I didn't do what you-know-who did"? Describe the circumstances. _____
_____
_____
_____
_____
_____

2. David met conviction with a change in behavior. The Holy Spirit always does His job, but we don't always do ours. If we do not fully submit to the Spirit's influence, we will often fight conviction. If we are filled by His Spirit, conviction will result in a change in behavior.

3. *David exercised great restraint.* He must have been influenced by the Spirit. He had the perfect chance to get revenge and he didn't take it! No one would have blamed him. He could easily have argued that his actions were in self-defense. Second Thessalonians 2:6-7 refers to the restraining work of the Holy Spirit. He is the One who holds us back when we are tempted to get revenge.

Have you ever been there—finally arrived at your chance to get a little justice and God wouldn't let you have it? If you recall an example, describe it in the margin. Don't share names or other information that would cause another person to be dishonored.

4. *David respected God more than he desired revenge.* Read 1 Samuel 24:6 again. Once more, why did David pledge not to lift a hand against Saul?

If you are willing to honor a person out of respect for God, you can be assured that God will honor you. The results of your obedience may differ, but the blessing of your obedience is guaranteed.

How do the following Scriptures encourage you to exercise restraint?

Ecclesiastes 3:17 _____

_____

_____

_____

_____

1 Peter 3:9 _____

_____

_____

_____

_____

Remember, the momentary opportunity for revenge might not only be a temptation from the evil one, but a test from God. Be ready in advance. No doubt the time will come when you will face a window of opportunity to get back at a person who has wronged you. The only way to get through a window God doesn't open is to break it yourself. This is one window sure to leave you injured. Don't do it. Let the Holy Spirit perform His restraining work. Someday you'll be glad you did.

Read 1 Samuel 25:39. Do you see any principles in this verse that could be applied in your future dealings with difficult people? ❑ Yes ❑ No If so, list them below.

_____

_____

_____

_____

_____

If you honor a person out of respect for God, God will honor you.

Scripture

You hear, O Lord, the desire of the afflicted; you encourage them, and you listen to their cry, defending the fatherless and the oppressed, in order that man, who is of the earth, may terrify no more (Ps. 10:17-18).

Discovery

You will discover that when you focus more on your situation than on God that problems appear bigger, you appear weaker, and God appears smaller.

Read 1 Samuel 27. The Philistines have been one of the greatest foes of the Israelites. Why would David settle in the land of the Philistines? _____
_____
_____

According to verse 1 what had David concluded at this point? _____
_____

Read verse 11. What exact reason is given for David leaving no one alive? _____
_____
_____

Life on the run obviously took its toll. Fear, frustration, and exhaustion apparently caused David to experience hopelessness, perhaps even depression and panic. Possibly he was driven to the point of paranoia. The result was a literal case of overkill. You can hear the downward spiral of his mood as you look closely at the first verse of the chapter: "One of these days I will be destroyed by the hand of Saul."

Read Psalm 10. Why did David feel as if God was far away and hidden in times of trouble? _____
_____

Which of the following words from Psalm 10:2 are ways David characterized his enemy?
❑ arrogant
❑ scheming
❑ dishonest
❑ mighty

In which of the following ways does David characterize himself as a victim?
❑ weak
❑ afraid
❑ sick
❑ grieved

Do you see what happens when we focus more on our battles than on God? Our enemy appears bigger, we appear weaker, and our God appears smaller. Beware! Long-term battles can cause vision impairment if eyes focus anywhere but up!

Have you ever battled an enemy so hard and so long that you felt like giving up or doing something crazy? _____
_____

Have you ever felt powerless over your real enemy and lashed out at someone who was completely innocent? _____

_____

_____

David's most obvious problem was that he felt so powerless and out of control in one area that he wielded an inappropriate amount of power and control in another area. We are also capable of responding destructively when we harbor similar feelings.

God has not forgotten. He has seen your battles. He knows those who have treated you unfairly. He knows when you're almost ready to give up or give in. Keep telling Him. Stay in His Word. Keep claiming His promises. We must stand in God's Word when the battles get tough and resist the temptation to panic.

Write the following verses in your own words.

Galatians 6:9-10 _____

_____

_____

_____

1 Peter 4:19 (Compare Peter's exhortation with David's in Ps. 10:14.) _____

_____

_____

_____

_____

Meditation

When was the last time you felt God was hiding Himself from you? What caused you to feel this insecurity in your personal relationship with God?

Read 1 Samuel 28.

Record the action Saul had previously taken according to 1 Samuel 28:3. "Saul had expelled the _____ and _____ from the land."

What did Saul want the woman from Endor to do for him? _____

_____

_____

According to the prophet Samuel, why did God refuse to answer Saul? _____

_____

_____

_____

Scripture

Our God is in heaven; he does whatever pleases him (Ps. 115:3).

Discovery

You will discover that no matter what's going on around you God is always in control.

Unconfessed, unrepented sin can easily be the reason for God's silence in our lives.

It is natural for us to personally feel the impact of God's occasional refusal to respond to the pleas of someone in His Word. At first we may wonder why God would not answer Saul since Saul first inquired of Him before he sought a spiritist.

Does God seem a little unfair to you at first in His lack of response to Saul? Why or why not? _____
_____
_____

God never responds haphazardly nor does He withhold an answer without regard. Why is God silent at times? Isaiah 59:1-3 gives us one very valid explanation for God's occasional silence–one which certainly applied to Saul at this time.

Read Isaiah 59:1-3 carefully then identify whether each of the following statements is true or false based on what you've read.
_____ **The arm of the Lord is too short to save.**
_____ **The ear of the Lord is not too dull to hear.**
_____ **Iniquities can never separate a person from God.**
_____ **God can choose not to hear the unrepentant sinner.**

Unconfessed, unrepented sin can easily be the reason for God's silence in our lives. Notice that Isaiah 59:2 does not say God can't hear, but that He won't.

Have you ever experienced the silence of God only to realize He was waiting for you to confront a sin in your life? Is there a sin you need to confess right now?

One prayer God will surely hear even when we've been rebellious and tried to do things our own way is the prayer of sincere repentance. The prayer for deliverance from sin must come before the prayer for deliverance from our enemies.

In Deuteronomy 18:10-12 what does God's Word say about spiritists and mediums? _____
_____
_____

Saul knew God's Word. Early in his reign as king he did what God's Word commanded. After his regard for God shrunk and his insecurities grew, he sought the very thing he once had considered wrong. We've done the same from time to time. We've felt convicted to get rid of something or to stop doing something; then, when our regard for God began to shrink and we tried to do things in our own insecure way, we were out the door hunting it down.

Read James 4:17. How does this verse apply to Saul? _____
_____
_____
_____

How does it apply to you and me? _____

_____

_____

_____

Let's be careful how much application we draw from this lesson about the dead. God did something very rare that day. He gave Saul a vision of Samuel raised momentarily from the dead so He could smack Saul in the face with His sovereignty. I don't want to mislead you. We cannot conclude from this encounter that our loved ones can ask God to let us appear to them after we're dead, or that it's okay for us to try to talk to the dead.

We see God's sovereign purpose for supernaturally intervening. The encounter ends with the harsh news of the imminent death of Saul and his sons. Sometimes the most merciful thing God can do in a rebellious person's life is let him know he is going to die so he can beg the mercy of God.

Read 1 Samuel 29:1–30:6. What two arguments did the Philistine commanders make against David to keep him out of battle?
❑ David might turn against them during battle.
❑ Achish showed favoritism to David.
❑ The battle would be too risky for David.
❑ David might attempt to regain Saul's favor.

David and his men returned to Ziklag after a three-day journey. What did they discover when they reached their destination?
❑ Ziklag had been raided.
❑ Ziklag had been burned.
❑ Their wives and children had been taken captive.
❑ All of the above.

Reread verse 6 carefully. Why would the men want to stone David? _____

_____

_____

_____

_____

David was greatly distressed over the blame his men cast on him. He responded by finding "strength in the Lord his God." What are a few things David might have done to find strength in his God? _____

_____

_____

_____

_____

I'd like to draw a few points from the verses we've just considered. The passage paints perfect portraits of human nature.

God sometimes delays the encouragement of others purposely so we will learn to find it in Him.

Meditation

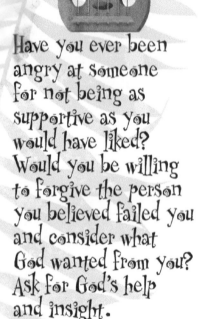

Have you ever been angry at someone for not being as supportive as you would have liked? Would you be willing to forgive the person you believed failed you and consider what God wanted from you? Ask for God's help and insight.

When God can bring about a victory and strengthen and mature us all at the same time, He's likely to do it!

1. Hurting people often find someone to blame. When we've suffered a loss, just like David's men we often look for stones to throw—and someone at whom to throw them. Notice that David also suffered the loss of his family. David cried the same tears the other men cried, but because they needed someone to blame, they focused their anger on him.

2. Nothing helps more than finding strength in our God. Sometimes no one offers us encouragement or helps us find strength. We'd better be prepared at times to strengthen ourselves in the Lord. Knowing how to encourage ourselves in the Lord is essential.

Without a doubt, the most precious and painful times I have had in this Christian experience were times when I realized I was all alone with God. Such times forge an unforgettable, inseparable bond. Don't miss the opportunity. I am convinced that God sometimes delays the encouragement of others purposely so we will learn to find it in Him.

Read 1 Samuel 30:7-31. When the victorious group returned conflict erupted over the plunder. What was David's apparent reasoning why they must all "share alike"? _____

_____

_____

_____

_____

_____

_____

Let's share a few words of application based on 1 Samuel 30:7-31.

1. Assured victory does not mean easy wins. God told David in advance he would "certainly overtake them and succeed in the rescue" yet we see references to exhaustion (v. 10), hard work (v. 17), a non-stop, 24-hour battle (v. 17), and four hundred escapees (v. 7). God often gives us a victory that requires blood, sweat, and tears. Why? Because He is practical. When He can bring about a victory and strengthen and mature us all at the same time, He's likely to do it!

God revels in overcoming and undergirding all at once. You see, God's idea of victory has virtually nothing to do with *plunder*. It has to do with *people*. *What* comes out of a battle isn't nearly as important as *who* comes out of a battle. That day God not only worked a victory *through* David. He worked one *in* David. The man after God's own heart came out of battle with grace and mercy and a little better grasp of God's sovereignty. God gave him the opportunity to participate firsthand in the fight.

2. We don't have to "win big" to win. No wholesale slaughter resulted. Quite the contrary, four hundred men got away, yet God called it a victory! We're going to win, but victory is going to take blood, sweat, and tears—His blood, our sweat, and tears from both of us.

When was the last time God brought you victory but the battle was difficult? __
_____
_____
_____

Describe what He accomplished in you through the difficult battle. _____
_____
_____
_____
_____

Thank God not only for what came out of the battle but who!

Read 1 Samuel 31. The first verse records the victory of the Philistines over Israel. Based on God's promise to Israel in Deuteronomy 11:22-25, why do you think Israel lost the battle? _____
_____
_____
_____

Why do you think the armor-bearer would not kill Saul? Record several possible reasons. _____
_____
_____
_____

What was Saul's final action?
❑ **He mourned the death of his sons.**
❑ **He killed himself with his own sword.**
❑ **He cried out to God.**
❑ **None of these.**

Scripture

When the armor-bearer saw that Saul was dead, he too fell on his sword and died with him (1 Sam. 31:5).

War is hard stuff, even when you're only a spectator. We're not well-acquainted with Abinadab and Malki-Shua, but we feel we've come face-to-face with the good, the bad, and the ugly in Saul and with the tender and beloved in Jonathan. I wonder if Jonathan had heard that David was on the other side. Did Jonathan look for David's face before he threw his spear for fear he'd harm his friend? Did Jonathan wonder if David intended to keep the covenant they had made even if Jonathan perished that day? Was he afraid? I find myself wanting to know more, not ready to find his name missing from the page. He was the kind of friend we all want—the kind of friend David needed.

The Philistines did not need Saul alive to mock him. They cut off his head, surely in memory of their slain giant, and impaled his body on the wall of Beth Shan. The valiant

Discovery

You will discover that God desires you to be His "permanent" servant, both worthy of honor and willing to give honor in God's name.

men of Jabesh Gilead heard the news and "journeyed through the night to Beth Shan." They removed the bodies and burned them. Two possibilities might explain the practice of cremation so rare among the Israelites: They were trying to remove all evidence of mutilation, or they were burning away the touch of the unclean hands.

The men of Jabesh Gilead paid a tribute to a king who started well. They showed their gratitude, even after 40 years. May we accept and imitate their example. May our memories of kindness be long and our memories of offenses be short. It's not too late to say thanks. Owe somebody a favor? How much better to repay it before you stand with them under the shade of a tamarisk tree.

Is there anyone you've never thanked appropriately for kindness done in your behalf? ❑ Yes ❑ No **If so, how could you show your appreciation?** _____

_____

_____

_____

_____

_____

_____

Saul saved the people of Jabesh Gilead, and the people remembered. Reflecting on things worth remembering deepens our relationship with our Savior. The Scripture references below mention several things we need to remember.

God's heroes are those who never forget His faithfulness.

Match each verse with the appropriate reminder.

____ A. Psalm 77:11   1. Remember, it is more blessed to give than to receive.

____ B. Psalm 89:47   2. Thank God upon your remembrance of a fellow believer.

____ C. Psalm 119:55

____ D. Acts 20:35   3. Remember how fleeting life is.

____ E. Philippians 1:3 4. Remember the miracles of God long ago.

5. Remember the Lord's name at night.

A good memory often leads the way to a good response. In the midst of a tragic scene, a group of heroes emerged, all because they had good memories. No doubt God's heroes are those who never forget His faithfulness. May we be counted among them.

Let's take a final look at the relationship between David and Saul. We've pictured the slain body of the first king of Israel, critically wounded by the Philistines, fatally pierced by his own sword. Nearby lay the body of his armor-bearer.

I'm not sure our current society has much to compare to the calling of an armor-bearer. Perhaps the closest we can come would be to study the lives of the secret service agents who guard the president. Recall the comparison we drew between ourselves and Jonathan's armor-bearer. We are the armor-bearers of God with one big difference: we don't just bear it, we wear it. As I kept thinking about that role and the body of the armor-bearer next to his king, God spoke a Scripture into my heart. It was Galatians 2:20.

Read Galatians 2:20 and explain what it means? _____
_____
_____
_____
_____
_____

Our old body of sin, the nature that must seek its own way, the person who is hopelessly depraved and resigned to failure, hangs limp on the cross. Raised in its place is the Spirit of the living God poured into a temple of flesh so that God's presence will remain among men. The armor that once could only be carried in our hands is now fitted for our frame and we rise from the dead—*warriors*. Oh, that we would not cling to the things of our old body of sin. It is nothing but a decaying carcass. I have been crucified with Christ. I no longer live but Christ lives in me. I must rise, turn away from the old things of death, take on His armor, and fight the good fight.

Write Romans 6:6. _____
_____
_____
_____
_____
_____

Paul assures us that our old self has been crucified with Christ. He intends that we no longer be slaves to sin.

Read 1 Peter 2:16. Write it here._____
_____
_____
_____
_____
_____

The word *servants*, which Peter is urging as the position of all who are in Christ, is the Greek word *doulos*. It means "a slave, one who is in permanent relation of servitude to another, his will being altogether consumed in the will of the other."[1] Sounds like an armor-bearer to me, doesn't it to you—sacrificing his will, his agenda, for the agenda of his master? The word *permanent* describes the kind of service God desires us to offer. In a society saturated with disposable razors, contacts, contracts, and marriages, the word *permanent* is like a lost treasure. Do you see your role of servant of the living Lord as absolutely permanent? I'm not talking about your salvation. I am talking about servant-hood. Can you say without a doubt, "I don't know where I will live in 20 years, whether I'll still have my health, a job, godly friends, or a growing church, but I can promise you one thing: I will be actively serving God"? If, with some sense of confidence, you can say those words, you are rare. You understand something of the role of a true *doulos*, a "sold out servant."

The word *permanent* describes the kind of service God desires us to offer.

Meditation

Have you ever experienced a loss only time could heal? If your answer is yes, how much time passed before you started to sense God's healing?

From the following Scriptures, what do you learn about servanthood that parallels the life of a loyal and true armor-bearer of God?

Galatians 1:10 _____
_____
_____
_____

Romans 14:4 _____
_____
_____
_____

With our role as God's servant/armor-bearer more deeply clarified, let's look at the first chapter of 2 Samuel.

Read 2 Samuel 1:1-27. Describe David's apparent feelings toward Jonathan in his expression of grief. _____
_____
_____
_____
_____
_____
_____

In David's song of lament, his words suddenly turn from a public address to the grief of a single heart: "I grieve for you, Jonathan, my brother." The original Hebrew word for *brother* in this verse was `ach. It meant "a brother, near relative. `Ach is any person or thing which is similar to another. It is generally a term of affection."[2] One was a shepherd, the other a prince, yet so alike were they, they were "one in spirit" (1 Sam. 18:1). They were brothers.

I know what it's like to lose a best friend. My buddy and I were absolutely inseparable. We dressed alike, cut our hair alike, shared a locker, and had endless sleepovers. I had lots of friends as a teenager, but I only had one best friend. Her name was Dodie. One day she dropped by the house to pick me up for a bite to eat. My parents would not let me go because we were preparing to leave town. Dodie never came back. Within half an hour, I heard the blood-curdling screams of an ambulance. I can hardly share it even today. I still visit her grave. I still ache for our friendship.

_____

[1] Spiros Zodhiates, *The Complete Word Study Dictionary: New Testament* (Chattanooga, TN: AMG Publishers, 1994), 483.
[2] Spiros Zodhiates, *The Complete Word Study Old Testament* (Chattanooga, TN: AMG Publishers, 1994), 2300.

Chapter Four
RIGHT PLACE

Sometimes God reveals Himself through
experiences we don't understand.

The war between the house of Saul and the house of David lasted a long time. David grew stronger and stronger, while the house of Saul grew weaker and weaker (2 Sam. 3:1).

Second Samuel 1 concluded as David received the tragic news of the death of Saul and his sons. David's life was destined to change dramatically. He was forced to grow up in a hurry and learn to make harsh decisions. David, a thinker, revealed his introspective, insightful spirit in the Psalms. We can see ample evidence of a man after God's own heart as we, too, reflect on the years between his anointing and the death of his predecessor. He had taken some wrong turns and some right turns, but he took virtually every step crying out to his God. As 2 Samuel 2 unfolds, David is 30 years old. Let's see what transpires "in the course of time."

Read 2 Samuel 2:1-7. Why did David go to Hebron? _____
_____
_____
_____

Discovery

You will discover that when you totally depend on God to use your struggles to accomplish His purposes, you will grow stronger.

How greatly we could profit if we would take to heart David's example in the first verse. David inquired of God before he took a single step forward in his inevitable journey to the throne. Did you notice that David kept asking until he had a specific answer from God? He wanted to get to the throne God's way.

God speaks to us today through His written and completed Word. God will speak specifically to us through Scripture if we learn how to listen. God has taught a method to me that never fails. It may take time but it always works. The method I use consists of four general steps:

1. *I acknowledge my specific need for direction.* Example: "Lord, I have been asked to serve on the youth council. I need to know whether or not this council is Your will for my life at this time."
2. *I continue to pray daily and study His Word.*
3. *I ask God to help me recognize His answer.* God usually helps me recognize His answer by revealing how His Word and the Holy Spirit He has placed within me both agree on the matter.
4. *I ask for a confirmation if I have any doubt.*

But what if the Holy Spirit still hasn't given you an answer when the deadline comes? I usually assume the answer is no. What works for you? How do you most often receive specific direction from God? _____

_____

_____

_____

_____

_____

It is good for us to consider how God spoke to and led in the lives of Abraham, Moses, David, and many others in Scripture. Like them, we may be asked to abandon our lives to God long before we assume the position for which He called us. Over 15 years had passed. What better time for David to have declared: "Your kingdom is an everlasting kingdom, and your dominion endures through all generations. The Lord is faithful to all his promises and loving toward all he has made" (Ps. 145:13).

Few experiences offer the opportunity to reflect on the past like finally settling down and establishing some roots. David and his family had been on the move for a long time. In Hebron they finally got a chance to settle down.

Have you had to move around a lot? Are you now or have you ever been in a place where you could settle down and make some friends? How does it feel to finally settle into a home, school, youth group, or friendship? _____

_____

_____

_____

_____

_____

Were you able to see that God was faithful to meet your needs even though you moved around? ❑ Yes ❑ No

David was anointed king over the house of Judah. Although God had given this kingdom to David, David would still have to take it from the old regime. Old regimes rarely crumble without bloodshed. Think about the demise of Nazi Germany. New regimes rarely arise without bloodshed. Consider the American Revolution. Rich history is written on the pages of 2 Samuel depicting the end of an old regime and the beginning of the new. Just like America's history, Israel's history was often written in blood.

Read 2 Samuel 2:8–3:5. List names of the characters you encounter. Make note of any special descriptions or identifying information. _____

_____

_____

_____

_____

_____

_____

_____

Second Samuel 3:1 provides evidence that *time* plus *conflict* equals *change*. We are told that "the war ... lasted a long time. David grew stronger ... while the house of Saul grew weaker." You and I have fought some pretty tough battles in our journeys—battles with temptations, strongholds, doubts, and fears. Some of them have lasted a long time. No matter what the cause of our battles, time will pass and change will come. Just like David and the house of Saul, we will either grow *stronger* or *weaker*. We cannot remain the same after a severe and long battle. We rarely stay the same in times of war. We can't always choose our battles, but we can certainly make choices to affect our outcome. We want to learn to make choices that will cause us to grow stronger rather than weaker.

> **We cannot remain the same after a severe and long battle. We will either grow stronger or weaker.**

Look up each of the following references. Write a one or two word summary of each of our three enemies:

1. Galatians 5:15-16 _____

2. Ephesians 6:12 _____

3. 1 John 2:15-16 _____

> **Time plus conflict equals change.**

We will fight these enemies to varying degrees for the rest of our lives. Sometimes we become discouraged because we see no progress, but we can be assured that *time* plus *conflict* equals *change*. We want to change for the better so our battles will not be in vain.

Read Psalm 20:1-9. Fill in the blank according to verse 1: "May the Lord _____ you when you are in distress."

Meditation

Are you in a battle with Satan and the evil principalities, the world, or your old sin nature right now? Spend time with God, asking Him to help you grow stronger as you depend on Him to accomplish His divine plan.

We cannot pick fights or choose our own battles and expect God to get involved and fight for us.

When we trust in the name of the Lord our God, what will be the ultimate results of our battles according to Psalm 20:8? _____

_____

_____

_____

Fill in the blank according to Psalm 20:9: "Answer us when we _____."

Compare verses 1 and 9 of Psalm 20. Why does God want us to call on Him before He rescues us? _____

_____

_____

_____

David continually called on God to fight his battles for him. Consequently, David always knew whose hand had brought the victory. The battles God allowed David to fight were means toward a divine end. We cannot pick fights or choose our own battles and expect God to get involved and fight for us. But when *God* ordains or permits our battles to be used to accomplish a divine end and *we* depend on God through every sweep of our sword, we *will* grow stronger instead of weaker.

Read 2 Samuel 4:1-12. How did Mephibosheth become lame? _____

_____

Why did David have Recab and Baanah killed? _____

_____

_____

Violence breeds violence. No matter the country or corporation, when there is a power struggle the most important question seems to become, "Whose side are you on?" We're not likely to draw actual swords and thrust them into the bellies of our brothers and sisters in Christ, but how God must be grieved when we use the sword of the Spirit (Bible) to unnecessarily wound other Christians. The Word of God is to be used as a sword against the Evil One, not against our own brothers and sisters in Christ.

What are some ways the Bible might be used to hurt others? _____

_____

_____

_____

_____

Through this study and others you may have taken, you are increasing your knowledge of the Word of God. We do not desire to gain only head knowledge. We have entered into this particular study of His Word so that our hearts might be changed. We want a heart like His. As our knowledge of the Word increases, may our knowledge of how to use the Word also increase.

Write a prayer asking God to help you use His Word appropriately as you deal with your brothers and sisters in Christ. _____
_____
_____
_____
_____

David is about to experience the fulfillment of God's promise! As we witness a tremendous point in the life of David, we can assume his thoughts were swirling with many things, filling him with all sorts of emotions.

Read 2 Samuel 5:1-5. Verses 4-5 mention several important numbers. Identify the significance of each of the following:
Forty years _____
Thirty years _____
Thirty-three years_____
Seven years and six months _____

Don't miss the significance of David's age when he became king. In Israel, 30 years of age was significant for several reasons. According to Numbers 4:3 and 23, a Levite could begin his service to the Lord as a priest or servant at age 30.

What further significance does the age of 30 possess according to Luke 3:23? __
_____
_____
_____

God is not concerned about age. David was a teenager when he killed the giant Goliath. He's looking for a willing, teachable spirit as He prepares us for service.

Look again at 2 Samuel 5:2. What did God call David to do in this wonderful affirmation of his commission? Fill in the blank: "And the Lord said to you, 'You will _____ my people Israel, and you will become their ruler.' "

Obviously a shepherd and a king have more than a little in common. God chose David in many ways because he was a shepherd! God often referred to Himself as a shepherd and His people as sheep. He also considered every earthly leader over His children to be a shepherd. (See Ps. 78:52-53; 100:3; 119:176; and Jer. 23:1.)

Scripture

Praise be to the Lord my Rock, who trains my hands for war, my fingers for battle. He is my loving God and my fortress, my stronghold and my deliverer, my shield, in whom I take refuge, who subdues peoples under me (Ps. 144:1-2).

God is not concerned about age. David was a teenager when he killed the giant Goliath.

Discovery

You will discover that sometimes we stand to learn the most about God from the situations we understand the least.

Meditation

Which of the names of God can you most readily call Him today? Can you call God by another name not listed in Psalm 144? Call God that name. Praise God for who He is.

Read 1 Peter 5:2-4. In what ways does God continue to draw an analogy to shepherds and sheep? _____
_____
_____
_____

Virtually all of us are leaders in some capacity. If you are involved in a student ministry or other church ministry, captain of a sports team, or Christian witness in your school, you are a leader. From David's successes and failures, we will learn volumes about leading people. He was God's choice and our example. Find out what happened after David became king over all Israel.

Read 2 Samuel 5:6-25. According to verse 10, why did David become "more and more powerful"? _____
_____
_____

David did not know how he would ever live to be king. But when God handed over the most fortified city in all Israel to David and placed favor in the heart of the king of Tyre toward him, David knew the Lord had established him!

You may be going through a confusing time right now. You may not know how God is going to use a situation in your life or why certain things have happened to you. But you can be encouraged and strengthened by recalling what you know about God in the midst of uncertainties.

Complete the following sentence as it applies to your life: I may not always know what God is doing in my life or why He works the way He does, but I always know ... _____
_____
_____
_____

In confusing times, recounting what we do know refreshes us. David still had many unanswered questions. He would never know for sure why God allowed certain things to happen, but he knew God had done exactly what He promised. You may never know why or how, but you can always know Who is faithful.

Strangely, David had come so far, yet he was back where he started. The hand that wrapped around his weapon as he waited for God's signal to overcome the Philistines looked far different from the hand that had searched for a smooth stone many years before. The first time he ever used his hands in battle was against the Philistines. Now he stood against them once more. To a man on the run, the Philistines had been a temporary refuge. They had taken advantage of his homeless estate by enjoying his strength. To a king on his rightful throne, they were clearly an enemy once more. Perhaps God inspired David to write the words of Psalm 144:1-2 on this very day.

God trained David for war, and only God could give him success. List every name David used for God in Psalm 144:1-2. _____

_____

_____

_____

Sometimes we stand to learn the most about God from the situations we understand the least.

David knew without a doubt that God had given him the victory and subdued the people under his leadership. He still didn't know why. He simply knew Who. Sometimes we stand to learn the most about God from the situations we understand the least.

Scripture

N ow we gather with the children of Israel on the city streets of Jerusalem as they celebrate the coming of their new king but not until we learn some difficult lessons. We will see that worship is not only the ultimate freedom and privilege but also an awesome endeavor to be taken seriously.

Read 2 Samuel 6:1-11. What did David and thirty thousand men set out to do?
❏ rebuild the tabernacle
❏ subdue the remaining enemies
❏ rebuild the city of Jerusalem
❏ bring the ark to Jerusalem

According to verse 3 how did they transport the sacred vessel? _____

_____

Scripture records two emotions David felt toward God after Uzzah was killed. What were they? _____

_____

_____

When have you felt these same emotions toward God? _____

_____

_____

_____

You turned my wailing into dancing; you removed my sackcloth and clothed me with joy, that my heart may sing to you and not be silent. O Lord my God, I will give you thanks forever (Ps.30:11-12).

Imagine becoming emotionally geared for a great celebration only to greet disaster instead. Uzzah's death would have been shocking under the most somber of circumstances, but can you imagine the shock in the midst of such celebration? David must have felt like he had emotionally jumped off a cliff.

Have you ever experienced devastation when you thought you were going to experience celebration? ❏ Yes ❏ No **If your answer is yes, what happened to turn your celebration into devastation?** _____

_____

Discovery

You will discover that worship is a freedom and privilege to be taken seriously.

David allowed his anger and fear to motivate him to seek more insight into the heart of God.

The more we learn about and the more we fear God, the more freedom we have to worship Him!

David felt anger and fear toward God, yet Scripture calls him "a man after God's own heart." I think one reason David remained a man after God's own heart was his unwillingness to turn from God, even when he felt negative emotions. David allowed his anger and fear to motivate him to seek more insight into the heart of God.

What does 2 Samuel 6:1-11 tell us about who God is? Scan the text one more time. Record any words used to describe God in these 11 verses. _____
_____
_____
_____

God is not trying to tell us He is harsh in these verses. He's trying to tell us He is *holy*. The words represent a big difference, although sometimes our limited understanding leads us to confuse them. The key to viewing the ark correctly is found in verse 2.

Now, based on who God is, can we draw any conclusions about what He was doing that day? I believe we can.

1. God was setting ground rules for a new regime. God was ushering in a new kingdom with a new king He had chosen to represent His heart. Remember that God does not look on the outward appearance, but on the heart.

2. God wanted His children to be different from the world. God would not accept attitudes and approaches from His children that were no different from the attitudes and approaches of the godless.

Read 1 Samuel 6:7-8. How did the Philistines transport the ark? _____
_____
_____
_____
_____

Do you see what Israel had done? They had copied the methods of the Philistines many years before when they returned the ark to the Israelites. How careful we must be not to think that God is less holy because others seem to get away with irreverence!

3. God wanted His kingdom to be established on His Word. The Israelites had made the mistake of transporting the ark by the same method as the Philistines without consulting God's designated commands for its transportation.

4. God was teaching the relationship between blessing and reverence. God desires His presence and His glory to be a blessing, but reverence for Him is the necessary channel.

Hard lessons learned well undoubtedly usher in a fresh respect and new freedom. As strange as this statement may seem, the more we learn about and the more we fear God, the more freedom we have to worship Him!

Read 2 Samuel 6:12-23. Michal insulted David for dancing before the Lord. Has anyone ever made fun of you or insulted you because of your outward expression of love for God? ❑ Yes ❑ No **If so, how did you feel?** _____

_____

_____

_____

_____

_____

_____

The following points can be taken from 2 Samuel 6:12-23:

1. *All worship is based on sacrifice.* Just as our bold approach to the throne of grace could only have followed Christ's shed blood on Calvary, David's bold approach that day in Jerusalem could only have followed the shed blood of sacrifice.

2. *Worship with abandon is an intimate experience.* We see David almost oblivious to everyone around him, totally free in the spirit, dancing through the streets of Jerusalem "with all his might" (v. 14)! We have gone with him from anger to rejoicing; from devastation to celebration.

God is not harsh; He is holy. He is not selfish; He is sovereign. He is not unfeeling; He is all-knowing. Like David, we need to come to know Him and respect Him and like David, we will love Him more.

Read 2 Samuel 7:1-17. Fill in the blank according to verse 1: "The king was settled in his palace and the Lord had given him _____ from all his enemies."

What concern did David share with the prophet Nathan? _____

_____

_____

_____

_____

_____

It is important to take times to rest our minds as well as our bodies. Have you ever studied really hard for a test and then days after the test what you studied starts to make sense? It is easy to get so caught up in studying that we miss the importance of what we are studying. David finally had time to take a break and that is when he noticed what was really going on around him. Once David took the time to notice, God revealed some awesome promises through the prophet Nathan.

God issued several wonderful and significant promises through the prophet Nathan in verses 9-16. Some were to David personally. Others were to the nation of Israel as a whole, and several were to David's "offspring."

God is not harsh; He is holy. He is not selfish; He is sovereign. He is not unfeeling; He is all-knowing.

Meditation

Are you aware of something God wants to give you or do for you? If so, what is it? How will you respond to God? Respond now.

In the columns below, record the promises under the appropriate headings:

To David	To Israel	To David's offspring

The prophet Nathan emerges as a new figure in Israel's history. God sovereignly raised prophets to serve as His voice to Israel. God apparently never intended for civil leaders to have absolute and unquestioned authority. They were to listen to the voice of God through His Word and through His prophets. All persons have someone to whom they must ultimately answer—parents and children alike; employees and employers alike; kings and kingdoms alike.

King David sought the counsel of Nathan, and in doing so revealed another important virtue: accountability. David did not consider himself to be above reproach or the need for advice. The statement David made to Nathan assumed the question, "What am I to do about the ark?" His sudden sense of concern urged him to be accountable.

Read James 5:16. Is there anyone to whom you confess your faults and seek counsel when you feel you have offended God? ❑ Yes ❑ No **If so, does this person offer godly counsel?** ❑ Yes ❑ No

Sometimes even a fellow believer can offer wrong advice. We are wise to make sure a fellow believer's advice agrees with God's Word.

What was Nathan's first response to David? _____
_____
_____
_____

Good ideas and God's ideas are often completely different.

The Lord can be "with" a person while a person can make a decision "without" God.

Look at what God taught both men.
- To David God said, "Don't assume that every bright and noble idea in a godly man's mind is of Me." Good ideas and God's ideas are often completely different.
- To Nathan God said, "Don't assume that a leader I have chosen is always right." The Lord can be "with" a person while a person can make a decision "without" God.

God's message to His new king was so rich, so revelational! He begins with a gentle rebuke, one we must remember every time we have a good and noble idea: "Are you the one to build me a house to dwell in?" In other words, "David, have I appointed you to do that?" God reminded David that He is fully capable of appointing a servant for specific tasks. If we are seeking Him through prayer and Bible study, we will not likely miss His appointments. We need to wait on God even when we have a great plan.

The climactic point in God's message to David comes in verse 11. Allow me to paraphrase: "David, you won't build a house for Me. I'm going to build a house for you!"

David discovered what we will often discover: You can't "out give" God. The covenant rested on God's faithfulness, not man's.

Read 2 Samuel 7:18-29. Fill in the blank according to 2 Samuel 7:18: "Then King David went in and _____ the Lord."

Have you ever responded like David? Have you experienced a time when someone told you something you knew was an answer from God, and you wanted to run as fast as you could and talk to Him? If so, when? _____

Record David's words in verse 18. _____
_____
_____
_____
_____

Read 2 Samuel 7:23-24 carefully. List every distinction for which David praises Israel. _____
_____
_____
_____
_____
_____

We often try so hard to blend in. We sometimes resent that God has ordained His "very own forever" people to seem strange to the rest of the world. Yet so much of our identity is based in our peculiarity!

Read 1 Peter 2:9. Have you ever felt different because you are a Christian? Explain. _____
_____
_____
_____

Read 2 Samuel 7:27 carefully. How do you think David found the courage to offer God his prayer? _____
_____
_____
_____

We need to wait on God even when we have a great plan.

Scripture

David reigned over all Israel, doing what was just and right for all his people (2 Sam. 8:15).

As Christians, so much of our identity is based in our peculiarity!

Discovery

You will discover that as God's child your identity is found in the character of His Son and the virtues reflected in His life.

I believe David was referring to his request for God to establish the house of David forever. He would never have prayed this prayer without first being told the will of God. David concludes his prayer with the words, "Now be pleased to bless this house." In other words, "Go ahead and do as You've so generously promised!" David was saying "Amen" to God's promises. David believed God, and he immediately began to pray accordingly, and with anticipation. Psalm 106:12 says, "Then they believed his promises and sang his praise."

Read 2 Samuel 8:1-18. Write in one sentence what you believe the point of this chapter to be. _____
_____
_____

Fill in the blank according to verse 13: "David became _____ after he returned from striking down eighteen thousand Edomites in the Valley of Salt."

Second Samuel 8 undoubtedly represents the height of David's career. God had given him success. David had it all: fame, fortune, power, and position. For just a little while, David handled the assured blessings of God with brilliant integrity. Let's seize the moment. We can identify the following virtues from our reading:

1. A spirit of cooperation. In 2 Samuel 7:10-11, God had promised David that He would give the nation of Israel rest from her enemies. David did not sit on the throne and simply wait for God to fulfill His promise. He obeyed God's call to the battlefield to participate in the victory!

Meditation

Reflect on the virtues of Christ as illustrated in the life of David. What virtues of Christ do you display in your own life?

Where do you believe you fit on the following scale in reference to having a cooperative spirit toward God?

Uncooperative   **Very Cooperative**

2. A ray of hope. David did not annihilate his enemy, leaving the nations destroyed. The reason was because he had not been told by God to do so. Secondly, I believe his God-given motive was to bring the other nations to a place of dependence and submission rather than a place of non-existence.

3. A literal dedication to God. At this point David had never confused the source of his strength. Any return from his feats he immediately dedicated to the Lord. If he was praised for his successes, he quickly gave the praise to God. If he was exalted for his successes, he lifted the name of God even higher. When he was surrounded by splendor, he wanted God to have something more splendid.

4. Justice and righteousness. We will consider the two virtues of justice and righteousness together. In His Word, God often treats them as a pair.

Justice and righteousness bring a specific response in the heart of God. Identify the response by filling in the following blank according to Jeremiah 9:24: "Let him who boasts boast about this: that he understands and knows me, that I am the Lord, who exercises kindness, justice and righteousness on earth, for in these I _____."

The characteristics God saw and loved so much in David are those most like His Son.

We have grasped David as a man after God's own heart. We've seen Christ's own heart illustrated over and over. No one was more humble. No one held Himself more accountable to God. No one revealed a greater heart for worship. No one had such a depth of cooperation with God. In all these ways David provides a picture of Jesus. Christ dedicated His every treasure to God, His Father, and will return for us when the Father nods. He will rule in justice and righteousness. As Chief Administrator, He will delegate the responsibilities of the kingdom to the faithful on earth. The characteristics God saw and loved so much in David are those most like His Son. God has one specific preference related to partiality: He loves anything that reminds Him of His only begotten Son. To be more like Christ is to be a man or woman after God's own heart.

To be more like Christ is to be a man or woman after God's own heart.

Read 2 Samuel 9:1-13. Whose kindness did David want to show according to verse 3? _____
_____
_____

What two ways did David want to show kindness to Mephibosheth for the sake of his father, Jonathan? _____
_____
_____

Correct the following statement based on verse 11. Draw a line through the error and supply the correct words: "Mephibosheth ate at David's table like one of his honored guests."

Scripture

David asked, "Is there anyone still left of the house of Saul to whom I can show kindness for Jonathan's sake?" (2 Sam. 9:1).

Don't you love God's Word? How I praise Him that His Word is not just a book of rules and regulations, do's and don'ts. The Bible is a book of the heart! You realize that God's Word reflects His ways as you read a story like the one we've read in 2 Samuel 9. His heart must be so tender.

David knew well the familiar feeling we all know as loneliness. He missed his best friend Jonathan and wanted to remember him in a special way. In the encounter between David and Mephibosheth we see several characteristics of God displayed. Consider with me the following virtues of God.

1. God's loving-kindness. David was searching for someone of the house of Saul to whom he could show God's kindness, not his own (v. 3).

The Lord is first of all kind. He is compassionate. God wants to deal with us first in mercy.

*2. God's **initiation of the relationship**.* "Where is he?" David inquired. Then he summoned Mephibosheth immediately. Note that Mephibosheth did not seek David. David sought Mephibosheth!

Read each of the following Scriptures. Note how David's action in seeking Mephibosheth shows God's action in seeking and loving us.

Luke 19:10 _____
_____

John 15:16 _____
_____

1 John 4:19 _____
_____

God looks for someone who will receive His loving-kindness.

God calls us just the way we are.

God is always the initiator of the relationship, always looking for someone who will receive His loving-kindness.

*3. God's **complete acceptance**.* David did not hesitate when Ziba informed him of Mephibosheth's handicap. How reflective of the heart of God! So many wait until they can get their act together before they approach God. If only they could understand, God calls them just the way they are; then He empowers them to get their act together!

What does Matthew 9:12 tell you about the heart of God? _____
_____
_____

Picture the scene when David met Mephibosheth. Imagine the king sitting on the throne, surrounded by splendor. His brightly adorned servants open the door, and before him stands a crippled man. With crippled legs he crept before the king, then he bowed before him! Mephibosheth was obviously humiliated. Have you ever felt like Mephibosheth? I have. Surely everyone who has ever accepted Christ as Savior has crept before Him, crippled from the fall of sin, overcome by our unworthiness against the backdrop of His Majesty's brilliance. "To the praise of the glory of his grace, wherein he hath made us accepted in the beloved" (Eph. 1:6, KJV)!

*4. God's **calming spirit**.* As Mephibosheth practically came crawling before the king, David exclaimed, "Mephibosheth!" He knew him by name … just as Christ knows us: "The watchman opens the gate for him, and the sheep listen to his voice. He calls his own sheep by name and leads them out" (John 10:3). David's next words were, "Don't be afraid." How many times have we seen those words come from the precious lips of our Lord: "It is I. Don't be afraid"?

5. God's delight in restoration. "I will restore to you all the land that belonged to your grandfather" (v. 7). David's first desire was to restore Mephibosheth. He had been so hurt by the fall. He had lived with such shame. The king could hardly wait to see Mephibosheth's shame removed and his life restored. David knew about restoration. He penned the words, "He restores my soul" (Ps. 23:3). Perhaps the most grateful response we could ever offer God for our restoration is to help another be restored.

6. God's desire for another son. Mephibosheth came stooped as a servant before the king. The king came before Mephibosheth to make him a son. He was family—invited to sit at the king's table to fellowship with him as one of his own! Imagine the sight when he first limped to the table set with incredible edibles, surrounded by festive activity, and sat down, resting his crippled legs at the king's table. Hallelujah! We are like Mephibosheth! No matter how many sons the Father has, He still wants more to conform into the image of His first and only begotten Son!

That's us, all right. One day, when we sit down to the ultimate wedding feast, the lame will be healed, the blind will see, the restored will leap and skip with ecstatic joy! We will be surrounded by the ministering servants of heaven! He is a God of loving-kindness. He's just searching for someone with whom to share it. Not just the moment when we first bow before Him and acknowledge that He is king, but every single time we sit at His table. Joint heirs. Sons. Daughters.

How does the story of Mephibosheth describe you? _____

_____

_____

_____

Read 2 Samuel 10:1-19.

Believe it or not, the account of this raging battle is filled with many virtues of David, each one further representing the God who chose him and placed his Spirit on him. I would like to highlight three outstanding evidences of God's character at work in David.

1. An active sympathy for the suffering. David knew better than anyone that a crown did not make a person void of feelings and oblivious to losses. David had experienced devastation. He had also been in need of sympathy.

Read the words of David in Psalm 69:20: "Scorn has broken my heart and has left me helpless; I looked for sympathy, but there was none, for comforters, but I found none." What happened when David looked to people for sympathy? _____

_____

_____

_____

_____

Discovery

You will discover that God is always the initiator of the relationship, always looking for someone who will receive His loving-kindness.

Perhaps the most grateful response we could ever offer God for our restoration is to help another be restored.

Meditation

Have you had a specific experience which has directly caused you to become more sympathetic to others? If so, reflect on the experience and ask God to show you how it can impact your personal opportunities to minister to others.

Have you ever felt this way? Have you ever desperately needed someone to listen to you or show concern for you in some way but couldn't find anyone?
❑ Yes ❑ No **If so, when?** _____
_____
_____

David penned each of the following verses. How does he describe the sympathetic heart of God in each one?

Psalm 103:13 _____
_____

Psalm 116:5,15 _____
_____

Psalm 145:9 _____
_____

God is always sympathetic, but His sympathy is not always accepted.

According to Hebrews 4:15, how was Christ able to sympathize with us?_____
_____
_____
_____

Do you allow God to extend sympathy to you in your pain or loss or do you tend to reject His efforts? _____
_____
_____

Remember that Christ is the extension of God's sympathy to you. Allow Him to minister to you in your need.

2. A fierce protectiveness toward his own. David sent messengers to meet the men so they would not have to be publicly humiliated. David fiercely protected the dignity of his men. God is even more protective of us.

Ever since Satan exposed shame in the garden of Eden, God's redemptive plan has been to cover it and relieve man of the chains of shame. He did so by His own blood. David revealed qualities of his Father, God, when he immediately responded to the shame of his own people with a plan to restore their dignity. He evidenced the protectiveness of God.

3. A vengeance toward the enemies of his people and the mockers of his mercy. David did not just formulate a plan to spare the dignity of his men. He took on their enemy himself. God also takes on our enemies when we've been shamed.

How do each of the following verses prove God's defensiveness toward those who hurt or shame His children?

Lamentations 3:58 _____

_____

Isaiah 35:3-4 _____

_____

Matthew 18:6-7 _____

_____

Let me assure you, God can take on your enemy with far more power and might than you could ever muster. When someone persecutes you, Your Father takes the persecution very personally, especially when you are persecuted for obeying Him, as David's men were. The battle is the Lord's!

Any one of us could be a man or woman after God's own heart. God is looking for qualities that remind Him of His Son, the object of His most supreme affections. These qualities are developed in us at no small cost, just as they were in the life of David; but the pleasure of God is worth it!

Which one of David's virtues is most outstanding to you? Explain why. _____

_____

_____

_____

_____

_____

_____

_____

God can take on your enemy with far more power and might than you could ever muster.

God is looking for qualities that remind Him of His Son.

Chapter Five

WRONG TIME

God always watches and waits with open arms for
His prodigal child to return.

Scripture

Blessed is he whose transgressions are forgiven, whose sins are covered. Blessed is the man whose sin the Lord does not count against him and in whose spirit is no deceit (Ps. 32:1-2).

Through many chapters of Scripture we've applauded the qualities of David. We've seen him as a devoted friend, loyal servant, courageous warrior, compassionate leader—truly a man after God's own heart. Verse after verse has attested to David's honesty, integrity, and accountability. Now in just a verse or two we see him tumble headlong into the pit of sin. Join me as we step out on the roof of an ancient Hebrew home to catch a breath of spring air.

Read 2 Samuel 11:1-5. Read verse 1 carefully. What was David supposed to be doing in the spring?
❑ celebrating the passover
❑ going off to war
❑ building the temple
❑ taking a census

David's temptation resulted in three specific actions recorded in verses 3 and 4. What are they?

1. _____
   _____
2. _____
   _____
3. _____
   _____

We may wish we could get everything we want until we look at David and Bathsheba. The gap between wanting and getting is where we must exercise self-control to protect ourselves. David had risen to a position where his every wish was someone else's command. David had ceased to hear a very important word—one without which integrity cannot be maintained. The word is *no*.

Have you recently had to say no to yourself for something you wanted but knew you shouldn't have? ❑ Yes ❑ No How difficult is it for you to say no? _____

_____
_____
_____
_____

What does God tell us "above all" about the heart in the following verses?

Proverbs 4:23 _____
_____
_____

Jeremiah 17:9 _____
_____
_____

Look at some of the conditions that led to David's sin.
1. *He was in the wrong place at the wrong time.* David had delegated so much responsibility that he left himself open to boredom and temptation.

2. *He failed to protect himself with people that held him accountable.* All of us need to surround ourselves with people who hold us accountable and who will question the questionable.

Discovery

You will discover that when your heart is far from God temptation will lead to sinful thoughts, words, and deeds.

Integrity cannot be maintained apart from one word: *no*.

How could an accountability partner make you stronger?_____
_____
_____
_____
_____

3. *He was lonely.* Dave Edwards, a well-known Christian speaker, once said, "All rebellion begins in isolation."

Reread 2 Samuel 11:1-5 and note three progressive areas of sin.

Step 1: He sinned in thought. First of all, David saw the woman bathing, then concluded she was very beautiful. Sight turned into desire. The seed of sin was first sown in his mind as he chose to stay on the rooftop, just as the seed of sin is first sown in our minds.

Read Mark 12:30. What does loving the Lord your God "with all your mind" mean? _____
_____
_____
_____
_____

Step 2: He sinned in word. Think how often sin that is not stopped cold in the mind makes its way to the mouth. If we begin to lust after something or someone and do not allow God to stop the thoughts, we'll start talking about it in one form or another just as David did. Talking draws us closer to action. Temptations rarely go from the mind to the deed. The second stop is usually the mouth.

Step 3: He sinned in deed. David flirted with adultery in thought and word, stopping at no point along the way to repent and ask God for help. Action followed. David committed adultery and set in motion a hurricane of consequences.

If wrong thoughts give way to wrong words, often giving way to wrong actions, how can we protect ourselves from wrong actions? _____
_____
_____
_____
_____

We must learn to allow God to stop sin in the place where it begins—our thought life! We are wise to aggressively confess the sins we think! Our thought life is so full of sins that their familiarity tends to make them less noticeable. Jealous thoughts, sudden lusts, quick criticisms, and harsh judgments may grow in our minds without us ever considering them as sin. God commanded us to love Him with our whole minds!

Write the following Scriptures in the space provided. Let them become a normal part of your prayer time to guide you through purity of thought, word, and deed before God.

Thoughts - Psalm 139:23-24 _____

_____

_____

_____

Words - Psalm 19:14 _____

_____

_____

_____

Deeds - Psalm 15:1-2 _____

_____

_____

_____

Two kinds of people are in greatest danger: Those who think they could never be tempted and those who are presently being tempted.

None of us is beyond any sin. Two kinds of people are in greatest danger: Those who think they could never be tempted and those who are presently being tempted. May we totally depend on the mercy of God and find help in our time of trouble. Particularly in *big* trouble.

Read 2 Samuel 11:6-27. Consider the words of verse 25, and describe David's heart at this point. _____

_____

_____

_____

_____

_____

_____

Considering the events we have read, David's heart was obviously further away from God than we imagined. We find four evidences of David's faraway heart.

1. David resisted many opportunities to repent of his sin and lessen the charges against him. We have all thrown ourselves into a revolving door of sin, just like David, and continued in a destructive cycle.

Why do you think David didn't stop and repent? You might consider the answer from a personal standpoint by asking yourself, "Why have I not at times stopped and repented in the earlier stages of sin?" _____

_____

_____

_____

We are dangerously far away when we can sin with little conviction.

Meditation

How near are you to the heart of God? Ask God to reveal to you where you are in your relationship with Him. Pray and commit to keep your heart near to God.

David was a man with God's Spirit in him! You can be assured the Spirit was doing His job of conviction! He had many opportunities to repent. Sadly, David had quenched the Spirit to such a degree that he resisted conviction over and over again. We are dangerously far away when we can sin with little conviction.

2. *David was unmoved by Uriah's integrity.* His faraway heart was unaffected by an encounter with authentic integrity.

3. *David tried to cover his own sin.* David was trying to cover his tracks. God wanted to cover his sins. Most of us have tried to cover our sin at one time or another.

Have you ever gotten tangled in a web of sin while you tried to cover the first sin that started it all? ❏ Yes ❏ No **What emotions did you feel during this time in your life?** _____
_____
_____

Who is blessed according to Psalm 32:1? _____
_____

Who did God inspire to write Psalm 32? _____

4. *He involved many others in his sin.* We, too, can become so self-absorbed we do not care what we are asking from others. Notice the contrast of hearts.

Indicate where you are in your relationship with God. Place an X on the line.

A heart far away from God. Characterized by extreme selfishness and self-absorbency.

A heart near God. Characterized by Christs' selflessness.

Read 2 Samuel 12:1-14. Why did Nathan use an analogy involving sheep? _____
_____
_____
_____

What was David's response to Nathan's analogy?
❏ He became angry.
❏ He believed the man deserved to die.
❏ He commanded he pay four times over.
❏ All of the above.

Fill in the blank according to the first part of verse 7, "Then Nathan said to David, _____."

At what point did David admit his sin? _____
_____
_____
_____

T his chapter is difficult and painful. The scene unfolds with Nathan sent to confront David's sin. We need to be careful not to confront for any other reason. We need to resist self-appointed confrontation with a Christian who has sinned. Galatians 6:1 records one of those reasons.

According to Galatians 6:1, who should restore a fallen brother or sister and why should he be careful? _____
_____
_____
_____

Nathan was God's man for the job, but he still needed the protection and leadership of God as he confronted the powerful, persuasive king.

Have you ever had unrepentant sin in your Christian life? ❏ Yes ❏ No How did it affect you until you repented from the sin? _____
_____
_____
_____

Read Psalm 32:3-5. What obvious toll did David's unwillingness to repent have on him? _____
_____
_____
_____

Psalm 32:3-5 teaches us an important truth. Spiritual illness (unrepentance) can lead to emotional illness (groaning all day, heaviness all night) and physical illness (bones wasted away, strength sapped). Please do not misunderstand. Certainly not all emotional and physical illness is caused by an unrepentant heart, but a continued refusal to repent can take a serious emotional and physical toll. I know. I've been there.

David placed God in an excruciating position. As God's foremost teaching instrument, even the eyes of the heathen nations were on David. God was teaching the way to the Messiah through His chosen king. Through David's victories, God taught something of Himself. Now, through David's failures, God would reveal something more of Himself. God's actions regarding David's sin teach the very foundation of all salvation—God will forgive the sinner, but He will still judge the sin.

Scripture

David burned with anger against the man and said to Nathan, "As surely as the Lord lives, the man who did this deserves to die! He must pay for that lamb four times over, because he did such a thing and had no pity." Then Nathan said to David, "You are the man! This is what the Lord, the God of Israel, says: 'I appointed you king over Israel, and I delivered you from the hand of Saul' " (2 Sam. 12:5-7).

God will forgive the sinner, but He will still judge the sin.

Discovery

You will discover that God loves you. He will discipline you, but He will always seek to draw you back to a place where He can bless you again.

Read 2 Samuel 12:15-25. Imagine yourself in David's position after his painful loss. Read his immediate responses in verse 20. Which response would have been most difficult for you and why? _____
_____
_____
_____

David knew something about his God that we need to realize as well. God did not create man in His own image to be unaffected by Him. More than any other creature, we are products, not of His head, but of His heart. Numerous times in Scripture God responds to the needs of His people with the words, "I have heard your cry." I would live in despair if I believed God is unaffected by our cries. The God of Scripture is One who feels.

Draw a line matching the following Scriptures to the emotional responses of God the Father, Son, or Holy Spirit.

Psalm 59:8	anger
Psalm 95:10	weeping
Zephaniah 3:17	deeply moved, troubled
John 11:33	delight
John 11:35	laughter
Ephesians 4:30	grief

Unlike us, God is never compromised by His feelings, but He is touched by the things of the heart. When David heard that he would live but his child would die, he probably begged God to allow him to die instead. Can you imagine God being unaffected by a parent's painful pleas? You may be thinking, *But, Beth, God did not do what David asked. David's prayers didn't change a thing. Where is grace? Where is mercy? What changed?* Let's consider a few of the things that changed.

1. David's painful pleas forced him back to a crucial place of depending on God. God demands we depend on Him because only He can keep us safe. When we depend on Him, He takes care of us.

2. David's pleas would satisfy his spirit in the many months of mourning to come. As he grieved the loss, he needed to know he had done everything he could to prevent the child's death.

In your relationship with God, do you feel freedom to bring the desires of your heart to Him in prayer? ❑ Yes ❑ No How do you usually respond if He does not give you the desire of your heart? _____
_____
_____
_____
_____

3. David's pleas ultimately ensured his survival through the tragedy he and his wife would suffer. David's pleas returned him to intimacy with God. The return positioned him to make it through great loss with victory. David's restored relationship to God enabled him to comfort his grieving wife. When tragedy hits, if we cast ourselves on the Savior and rely on Him for the very breath we draw, we will one day get up again.

4. David's pleas touched the heart of God to respond. Out of grace God removed the curse on the sinful union of David and Bathsheba. Their union had been wrong. Their motive was wrong. But now we see them drawn together by terrible tragedy. God removed the curse of their marriage and brought a child from their union. *Jedidiah* means "beloved of the Lord."

"The Lord loved him." God loves you. He will discipline you, but He will not forsake you. He will always seek to draw you back to a place where He can bless you once more.

Read Psalm 51 aloud. In verses 10-12, what six requests of God did David make?

1. _____
2. _____
3. _____
4. _____
5. _____
6. _____

Meditation

Remember times when God has brought good things out of not so good situations. Thank God for always being faithful to show His love to you through times of discipline.

This Psalm invites the most wretched of sinners to drink from the fountains of forgiveness. Consider these specific phrases from each of the first 13 verses.

Verse 1: "Have mercy upon me, O God." David recognized that until he had expressed repentance, words would be wasted. "According to your unfailing love; according to your great compassion." At this moment, David called on the God of love and compassion. Only on the basis of God's promise of love could David dare ask for mercy.

Verse 2: "Wash away all my iniquity and cleanse me from my sin." The mercy of God is enough to cover all our sins.

Are you able to accept that all your confessed and rejected sins have been completely forgiven? ❏ Yes ❏ No If your answer is no, what do you think holds you back from accepting God's complete forgiveness? _____

_____
_____
_____
_____
_____

Scripture

Create in me a pure heart, O God, and renew a steadfast spirit within me. Do not cast me from your presence or take your Holy Spirit from me. Restore to me the joy of your salvation and grant me a willing spirit, to sustain me. Then I will teach transgressors your ways, and sinners will turn back to you (Ps. 51:10-13).

The biggest heartbreak over sin comes with the realization that we have offended God.

Verse 3: "For I know my transgressions." Psalm 51:3 proves David could not ignore his sins! Are you in David's position right now? Are you carrying the weight of past sin? Is the guilt and remorse more than you can bear? Do you have a sin you can't seem to give up? One you can't live with, but can't bring yourself to live without? The freedom of Christ is worth the surrender of absolutely anything!

Verse 4: "Against you, you only have I sinned." For those of us who have known God and experienced the presence of God, the biggest heartbreak over sin comes with the realization that we have offended Him. God takes our sin personally.

Verse 5: "Surely I was sinful at birth." David recognized something of the depth of his inclination to sin.

Verse 6: "Surely you desire truth in the inner parts." God is our one and only source of transforming truth. Deep inside in the secret places we are most vulnerable to lies.

"You teach me wisdom in the inmost place." Knowledge stamped on the heart makes one wise.

Verse 7: "Cleanse me with hyssop." For the people of the Old Testament, hyssop carried a powerful ritual and symbolic message.

"Wash me and I will be whiter than snow." Satan lies to you. He tries to convince you that you are covered by guilty stains even when you have long since repented.

Verse 8: "Let the bones you have crushed rejoice." God sometimes uses circumstances and discipline to figuratively break our legs from continuing on the path of sin.

Verse 9: "Hide your face from my sins." Allowing God to open our eyes to sin is not only painful but also embarrassing! Once we look, we don't want God to look. We must accept the fact that He's already seen our sin, still loves us, and wants to forgive us.

Verse 10: "Create in me a pure heart." David was admitting his need for something only God could do. A pure human heart is perhaps God's most creative work!

Verse 11: "Do not … take your Holy Spirit from me." To David, the removal of God's Spirit was a fate worse than death.

Verse 12: "Restore to me the joy of your salvation." Sometimes our prayers seem to go unanswered because, in our misery, we beg for our joy to be restored without the obedience of fully turning from our sin.

Verse 13: "Then I will teach transgressors your ways, and sinners will turn back to you." There is no more willing and effective evangelist and teacher than one who is humbled, cleansed, renewed, and restored.

Read 2 Samuel 13:1-22. People often say, "You can learn a lot about a person just by looking at his friends." What can you learn about Amnon by looking at his friend, Jonadab? _____

_____

_____

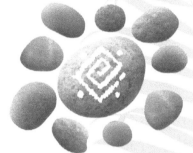

These verses are filled with tragedy. The focus of this corruption was a beautiful young virgin, daughter of the king, no doubt keeping herself pure for the man she trusted God would one day bring her. The events in chapter 13 are scandalous even by today's standards, and as painful.

If you have experienced shame I pray that you will allow God to bring you victory in the vulnerable areas of your life. God is faithful. God can get you through your grief. Getting through it may involve telling someone. Is God telling you to share what happened with someone who can help?

You will discover that God offers forgiveness to the most terrible of sinners.

Read 2 Samuel 13:23-39. What possible evidence could you offer to support the following statement: Absalom was counting on his father's unwillingness to attend his celebration? _____

_____

Do you see any evidence in verse 32 that the "shrewd" Jonadab might have played both sides of the conflict between Amnon and Absalom? Explain._____

_____

_____

Two years passed with bitterness multiplying in Absalom's heart. That's the nature of bitterness. It never stays in its cage. Absalom must have watched and waited to see if his father would call Amnon to account for his crime. His father didn't.

Absalom waited for an opportunity. He devised an elaborate scheme to summon Amnon to his house. The time of sheep shearing was a festive occasion with huge family celebrations. Absalom seized the opportunity, counting on his father to continue distancing himself from family obligations and celebrations. When David refused to come, Absalom requested Amnon's presence in his place, assuming no one would be suspicious. Customarily, the oldest son represented his father in the father's absence.

Jonadab reared his ugly head in another scandalous scheme. He would never have known Absalom's plans had he not become his confidant. I wonder if he ever told Absalom that he was the one who devised the scheme against Tamar. Not likely. The tragedy ends with one son dead, one son missing, and one father grief stricken. David had two responses toward Absalom after Amnon's death: he mourned for him and longed for him. Once again David feels the right thing and does the wrong thing.

If you are afraid to give up something you know is wrong for you, tell God about it. Confess your fears and let Him encourage you and fill you with His Word. Express your feelings and ask for His help.

Scripture

Like water spilled on the ground, which cannot be recovered, so we must die. But God does not take away life; instead, he devises ways so that a banished person may not remain estranged from him (2 Sam. 14:14).

Read 2 Samuel 14:1-33. Why did Joab devise a method somewhat like a parable to get through to David?_____
_____

Why did Joab refuse to come to Absalom when he summoned him? _____
_____
_____
_____

Absalom finally got Joab's attention. He set his field on fire. From his method of getting attention, what can you surmise about Absalom at this point?_____
_____
_____
_____

Was the meeting between David and Absalom what you expected or did you imagine their reunion differently? Explain. _____
_____
_____
_____
_____
_____

Discovery

You will discover that learning to forgive, even if no one takes responsibility for his or her actions, will save you from misery.

David granted Joab's request and allowed him to summon Absalom. Joab was so thrilled, he "fell with his face to the ground … and he blessed the king" (v. 22). He joyfully hastened to bring the young man home, no doubt picturing the emotional but wonderful reunion of this father and son. He brought Absalom back to Jerusalem, bracing himself and Absalom for the glorious reunion. He was met with these words from the king: "He must go to his own house; he must not see my face" (v. 24). I am very grateful God will not call us to the heavenly Jerusalem and say, "She must not see my face." I've waited all my life to see His beautiful face!

Where will we live in heaven according to John 14:2? _____

Fill in the following blank according to Revelation 22:3-4. "No longer will there be any curse. The throne of God and of the Lamb will be in the city, and his servants will serve him. _____ and his name will be on their foreheads."

David did not respond like the father of the prodigal in Christ's parable—the father who searched the horizon daily for his wandering son to come home. That father, who represents our heavenly Father, caught a glimpse of his son in the distance and "ran to his son, threw his arms around him and kissed him" (Luke 15:20).

Some things in life are do-overs. God sometimes gives us a second chance to do something right. Some chances never come back around. The chance for David and Absalom to be completely reunited in their hearts would not come again. By the time David finally received Absalom, his son's heart was cold.

Have you ever had a chance to be reconciled with someone but resisted?
❏ **Yes** ❏ **No If so, what were some of the reasons you resisted?** _____
_____
_____
_____
_____
_____

Did the lack of reconciliation cost you in any way? ❏ **Yes** ❏ **No If so, how?** ____
_____
_____
_____
_____
_____

God sometimes gives us a second chance to do something right.

God is never in the wrong when He and one of His children are separated; yet He devises ways so that His banished child may not remain estranged from Him. Never underestimate the significance of timing when it comes to mending. You may not get another chance.

Is there anyone to whom you need to be reconciled? If your answer is yes, what do you need to do to take the first step toward mending this relationship? ____
_____
_____
_____
_____

God is never at fault when He and one of His children are separated; yet He devises ways so that His banished child may not remain estranged from Him.

King David and Absalom finally saw each other face-to-face. Sadly, however, their reunion was too little, too late. We will see evidence of Absalom's deep dissatisfaction about his encounter with his father. Their meeting did nothing but fuel his bitterness. The relationship between David and Absalom teaches us an important object lesson: reuniting and reconciliation can be two very different things.

Read 2 Samuel 15:1-12. Explain what you think Absalom was trying to accomplish in verse 4. _____
_____
_____
_____
_____
_____
_____

Verse 6 states Absalom's motive and obvious success. Fill in the following blanks: "Absalom behaved in this way toward all the Israelites who came to the king asking for _____, and so he stole the _____ of the men of Israel."

According to verse 10, Absalom sent secret messengers throughout the tribes of Israel to say: "As soon as you hear the sound of the trumpets, then say Absalom is _____."

According to verse 12, Absalom tried not only to steal the hearts of the people but also to steal David's counselor, Ahithophel. Why do you think he might have wanted Ahithophel? _____
_____
_____
_____
_____
_____

Although people got mad, no one cleaned up the mess. Lives continued to be torn by the shrapnel no one ever swept away. David did not—perhaps could not—live up to Absalom's expectations. The results were devastating. The revenge he had taken on Amnon's life was not enough. The fact that his father still called him a son was not enough. He still cried out for vengeance and was determined his father would pay.

Have your parents ever let you down? If so, how did you deal with being let down? _____
_____
_____
_____
_____

Do you think you handled the situation correctly? If not, how could you have handled it better, in a Christlike manner? _____
_____
_____
_____
_____

Absalom spent two years waiting for David to punish Amnon, three years in hiding after killing Amnon, two years in Jerusalem waiting for David to receive him, and four years working his devious plan of vengeance against his father. Unforgiveness and retaliation stole eleven years of his life! Talk about something he couldn't do over! Eleven years is a long time for anyone to harbor bitterness.

Has anger or bitterness stolen years of your life? ❑ Yes ❑ No If so, estimate how many, if possible. _____

Has the bitterness or anger ended? ❑ Yes ❑ No **If your answer is yes, how did it finally end?** _____

_____
_____
_____

If your answer is no, why do you still feel bitter or angry? _____

_____
_____
_____

God tells us to forgive those who hurt us, but He never qualifies the command by saying forgive only when someone asks for your forgiveness. He simply says forgive (Luke 6:37).

Have you ever resisted forgiving someone who hurt you or disappointed you because the person never took responsibility for his or her actions and asked forgiveness? ❑ Yes ❑ No **Can you see any ways in which your unwillingness to forgive hurt you more than the person who injured you?** _____

_____
_____
_____
_____

Those who hurt us often have no idea how deeply we will suffer. If we follow Christ's example, we will be free. We can save ourselves a lot of heartache! Learning to forgive even if no one takes responsibility for his or her actions will save us from the kind of misery that ultimately destroyed Absalom.

Read 2 Samuel 15:13-37. What did David do when he heard the news of Absalom's conspiracy? _____

_____
_____
_____

There on the Mount of Olives, continuing up to the summit, an amazing thing happened: "David prayed" (v. 31). Little by little, things began to happen. David had run from his throne practically hopeless. "We must flee, or none of us will escape from Absalom" (v. 14). But somewhere on top of that mountain, David got down on his knees and prayed. See his prayer for yourself. God had him write it down. It's Psalm 3.

On the Mount of Olives where people used to worship, David confronted the Spirit of God who had grown accustomed to being honored there—still hovering—just in case someone might follow in the footsteps of old and worship once more. Someone did.

Meditation

Read Psalm 3. What impresses you about David's heart and state of mind as he wrote these words from God's holy hill?

God simply says, "forgive."

Scripture

"As he [David] went, he, said: "O my son Absalom! My son, my son Absalom! If only I had died instead of you—O Absalom, my son, my son (2 Sam. 18:33).

How do you define *worship*? _____
_____
_____

What is your favorite way to worship God? _____
_____

Take time to worship God right now.

❧

We drive further into the conflict between a refugee king and his embittered son. The conflict in the kingdom rekindled old supporters of Saul who were still nursing grudges against David.

Read 2 Samuel 16:1-14. For the sake of review, identify the following individuals. Look back at 2 Samuel 9 if necessary.

Mephibosheth: _____
_____

Ziba: _____
_____

Why wouldn't David let Abishai defend him against Shimei? _____
_____
_____
_____

Restate David's hope in verse 12: _____
_____
_____
_____

Have you ever noticed how mean-spirited people will kick a person when he's down? David had seemed invincible; yet the moment he appeared vulnerable, opportunists descended on him like vultures. David had suffered so much betrayal, he assumed no one was beyond turning on him.

Can you remember ever feeling like someone took advantage of you at a time when you were vulnerable? ❑ Yes ❑ No **If so, describe what happened without mentioning any names.** _____
_____
_____

Consider the timing of David's obstacle—just as David was regaining a shred of strength! Coincidental? No way! Just when Satan suspects we are regaining a spark of hope, he runs to greet us with discouragement and rejection. Notice David's response to Abishai's request to avenge David's persecution: "My son, who is of my own flesh, is trying to take my life. How much more, then, this Benjamite! Leave him alone" (v. 11). I believe David might have been saying: My own beloved son has rejected me. There is nothing anyone can do to injure me any more deeply. Let him go ahead. Maybe I deserve it.

I want to express something to you that I hope you'll receive with your whole heart: We can still cry out to God for help even when we think we're getting what we deserve. God comes to us even when our pain is self-inflicted. Times of humiliation and persecution do not have to be permanent injuries.

Many times God will send someone to encourage us when we are down. Think of a time when you have been down or in vulnerable circumstances. Who did God send to encourage you? _____

_____

_____

Read 2 Samuel 16:15–17:29.

God was there all along for David. We will have missed the turning point of the conflict between David and Absalom if we miss the importance of God "frustrating" Ahithophel's advice. Absalom's decision not to follow his counsel led to David's upper hand in the battle for the kingdom. Ahithophel was a traitor to his king. Note the parallels between David's betrayer and Christ's betrayer many centuries later. Ahithophel and Judas had things in common:
• Both were chosen members of a very important team.
• Both betrayed their masters and went with the crowd.

You and I have a "friend who sticks closer than a brother" (Prov. 18:24) for "Greater love has no one than this, that he lay down his life for his friends" (John 15:13). No matter what happens, no matter who rejects you or humiliates you, He will never betray you. Stay faithful, believer. You are on the winning team. The King of all kings will return and take His rightful throne.

We have watched an emotional match involving two opponents torn between love and hate. Now we will see one go down tragically. We can't change the story. We can only agree to be changed through the story.

Read 2 Samuel 18:1-18. Why do you think David might have wanted to lead the battle himself? _____

_____

_____

_____

Discovery

You will discover that sin has destructive consequences and hurts everyone it touches.

Just when Satan suspects we are regaining a spark of hope, he runs to greet us with discouragement and rejection.

We can still cry out to God for help even when we think we're getting what we deserve.

Why didn't David's men want him to go to battle? _____
_____
_____
_____

What strange accident happened to Absalom? _____
_____
_____
_____
_____

According to verse 18, what had Absalom done during his lifetime? _____
_____
_____
_____
_____

Absalom wasn't the first nor the last person to confront the cold, hard fact that life isn't fair. Some have experienced more harshness than others. No doubt you know someone who has faced—or is now facing—tragedy.

What have you or someone you care about experienced that you consider to be evidence that life is not fair? _____
_____
_____
_____
_____

Our response to difficulty becomes far more important than the hardship itself.

The real issue for us is not whether or not life is fair. The real issue is "How will I respond to the difficult and painful events that occur in my life?" Ultimately our response to difficulty becomes far more important than the hardship itself. The rape of Tamar seems to have launched Absalom on his path of destruction, but his response to the rape was the key. He had the choice to respond in wisdom or in bitterness.

We can only shake ourselves free so many times. If we keep flirting with disaster, we're finally going to get trapped. The picture of Absolom's death was the picture of his life: the noose of bitterness choking the captive's cry. In the end, those close enough to hear him choking no longer cared.

Read 2 Samuel 18:19-33. What did David say when he realized Absalom was dead? Write David's words from verse 33. _____
_____
_____
_____
_____

I wanted you to write the last words of chapter 18 so that your own hand and heart could experience the repetition of the words, "O Absalom, my son, my son!" Suddenly, a heart of tragically suppressed love exploded. Tears David should have cried long ago poured from his eyes. Words he should have said the moment he first saw his prodigal son finally burst from his lips: "My son, O, my Son!" He did not speak about him. He spoke right to him, as if his voice would carry to the depths of the pit where the body lay.

"If only I had died instead of you!"

Death would have been far easier than life without him. And where was God when David lost his son? Where was He when a king's own countrymen pierced his son? Where was He when the blood poured forth? The same place He was when He lost His own Son. God is always with us.

Meditation

Think back on a time when you were broken before God. When were you able to experience His joy again?

Scripture

He won over the hearts of all the men of Judah as though they were one man. They sent word to the king (2 Sam. 19:14).

Chapter Six

HURTING AND HEALING

God is faithful to finish the good work He started.

Chapter 5 concluded with the tragic death of the young prince Absalom and the broken heart of the aging King David. Divided loyalties left God's chosen nation in an upheaval. Our study will now focus on one chapter of Scripture, packed full of critical information and significant encounters.

Read 2 Samuel 19:1-14. Based on their responses to David's grief, how do you believe David's men felt about him? _____

_____

_____

_____

How would you characterize Joab's method of motivating David to get back to work? _____
_____
_____

How did the people of Judah accept David's message according to verse 14? ___
_____
_____
_____

Even though Joab's heart was wrong, David concluded that his advice was right. He returned to the business of the kingdom, but he decided to replace Joab with Amasa. David realized his army had fought in his behalf, and he must not have them return in shame. Verse 8 tells us he got up and took his seat in the gateway. The text proceeds with the words, "When the men were told, … they all came before him." The words represented a pivotal moment. The king became accessible once more. It had been a long time—far too long.

You will discover that God is true to His word and He expects you to be true to your word.

We've looked at David from many angles at this point in our study. Write four or five adjectives which you believe describe David. _____
_____
_____

Read 2 Samuel 19:15-30. What evidence do you see of Mephibosheth's loyalty to David and his innocence in spite of Ziba's accusations? (See 2 Sam. 16:3.) _____
_____
_____
_____
_____

I will never forget having a family picture taken at Thanksgiving after we had adopted our son, Michael. As I framed the new picture, he jumped up and down and exclaimed, "It's the whole Moore family, and not one of us is missing!" We had covered our house with his pictures, but I never realized how much the family picture that had been taken before he came had bothered him. One day God may take a family portrait in heaven. All of God's children—the natural born of Israel and the adopted sons and daughters, the church—will be there and not one of us will be missing.

Business as usual. The king crossed the Jordan with an entourage escorting him back to his throne, and before he could dry off his feet, his folks were in a fight. Some welcome home for our King David!

Read 2 Samuel 19:31-43. Have you ever recommitted yourself to a previous relationship or situation only to discover things had not changed much? ❏ Yes ❏ No
If so, when was it? _____
_____

Doing the right thing is rarely the easy thing.

How did you feel? _____
_____
_____
_____

Did you hang in there in spite of it all? ❑ Yes ❑ No **If so, what motivated you to work toward a positive end?** _____
_____
_____
_____

Returning to a former relationship or situation isn't always easy. Going home isn't always fun, especially when something unpleasant waits for you. Doing the right thing is rarely the easy thing. Although it was too late for Absalom, it was not too late for David. And it's not too late for you.

Read 2 Samuel 20:1-26.

Why did Joab kill Amasa? (Review 2 Sam. 19:13.)
❑ **Amasa had plans to betray David.**
❑ **David had given Amasa Joab's position.**
❑ **Amasa had violated David's orders.**
❑ **The families of Amasa and Joab had been enemies for generations.**

David should have known Joab was not going to clean out his desk and resign peaceably. He forced his way back into his former position by killing Amasa, the man David had chosen to replace him.

Another fact makes Joab's actions against Amasa considerably more horrible. Read 1 Chronicles 2:16-17 carefully. What was the relationship between Amasa and Joab? _____
_____

As the plot thickened in the twentieth chapter, one woman was willing to become more than a spectator to imminent disaster, and as a result of her intervention an entire city was spared. Just when we're about to throw up our hands over the unwillingness of people to get involved and help, out steps an authentic hero! An entire village could have perished because one person was such a troublemaker.

God expects His people to be true to their word so that those watching might come to believe that He is true to His word.

God provides two responses to broken vows: repent and recommit.

Do you know of someone who risked involvement in a community need or another's personal need and made a significant difference? ❑ Yes ❑ No **If so, describe the situation.** _____
_____
_____
_____
_____

Read 2 Samuel 21:1-14.

God meant for His people to be true to their word. He still does. Surely one reason He expects His people to be true to their word is so that those watching might come to believe that He is true to His word.

God considers vows extremely important. This is what he says in His Word: "It is better not to vow than to make a vow and not fulfill it. Do not let your mouth lead you into sin. And do not protest to the temple messenger, 'My vow was a mistake' " (Eccl. 5:5-6).

Many teenagers have taken vows of purity to God through a wonderful program called True Love Waits. You may be one of them. I spoke at a youth camp one summer in which several high schoolers came to me individually grieving over their broken vows. They asked my advice. I didn't have to think very long to answer, based on what I understand about God and His Word. I explained to them that I have also made promises to God along the way that I have not kept. But rather than continue to be disobedient, God provides two responses to broken vows: repent and recommit.

King David brought the bones of Saul and Jonathan from Jabesh Gilead to bury them in the family tomb. (See 2 Sam. 21:14.) He returned to Jerusalem to find that he would be forced to take back his throne, since it was apparent that it was not going to be offered to him willingly. One last enemy arose before he could take a breath and proclaim victory. One very familiar enemy. One very persistent enemy.

Read 2 Samuel 21:15-22. Why did David's men insist he not accompany them to battle any more? _____

_____

_____

_____

_____

Few things make us want to run away more than the prospect of having to fight an old battle. The moment that familiar enemy reappears, we want to run and never come back. Have you ever noticed how Satan always chooses just the right time to haunt you through an old enemy?

Satan is the counterfeit god of perfect timing. He's watching for just the right moment to pull the rug out from under us, but the rug is under God's feet. And God always has victory in mind! He will never allow Satan to discourage you without a plan to lead you to victory! We may not always follow Christ to victory, but He is always leading!

Meditation

Is there a vow you have made to God that needs a fresh dose of recommitment? If so, offer a prayer of commitment to God. Ask His help in fulfilling your vow.

Scripture

Once again there was a battle between the Philistines and Israel. David went down with his men to fight against the Philistines, and he became exhausted (2 Sam. 21:15).

We may not always follow Christ to victory, but He is always leading!

Write 2 Corinthians 2:14. _____
_____
_____
_____
_____

One of the most important truths we can apply from David's ongoing battles with the Philistines is that God will always lead us to victory and He will lead us His way. God led David to victory through all four of the battles recorded in 2 Samuel 21:15-22, but He brought the victory to David through someone else.

Read 2 Samuel 23:8-39.

God purposely brought victory to David through someone else on many occasions. Consider a few reasons why God might have used this method in the life of David.

1. For the sake of the people. Israel did not need David to be like a god to them. Nor could David deal with being put on that kind of pedestal or subjected to that kind of pressure. He was bound to disappoint his people. God is wise. He will never allow any of us to be the only one through whom He appears to be working mightily.

2. For the sake of King David. Remember what happened when David thought he had risen above his normal duties as a king and stayed behind in the spring when other kings went off to war? That's when the nightmare began! God gave David a few heroes—a few men who commanded his respect. He humbled David and made him depend on them for his life. None of us will escape this important life lesson. God will teach us dependency.

Read the following Scriptures. Describe how God may have been teaching David these same truths by allowing him to depend on others.

Philippians 2:3-4 _____
_____
_____
_____
_____

1 Corinthians 12:21 _____
_____
_____
_____
_____

3. For the sake of the men he empowered. People can easily be discouraged if they begin to believe that God works mightily through others but never works through them.

God does not play favorites. Anyone who cries out to Him, He answers. Anyone who surrenders to His call, He uses.

God has heroes. If you don't believe it, check Hebrews 11. You'll only find part of the list, however, because it just keeps getting longer and longer. The name of every surrendered person who endures by faith and not by sight is on it. No doubt some of your heroes are on that list. You may be surprised to find your name listed there as well!

List what you consider to be characteristics of a hero of the faith. _____
_____
_____
_____

Having heroes of the faith is fine. But remember, heroes aren't perfect. They simply live to serve and honor God. List a few of your heroes. Take time to thank God for them. _____
_____
_____
_____
_____

Read the following three questions before you read 2 Samuel 22:1-51. This will help you to identify some of the answers as you read the passage.

1. List every name, object, or role by which David refers to God:

_____   _____   _____
_____   _____   _____
_____   _____   _____

2. Which verses and phrases affirm that God blesses the obedient? _____
_____
_____
_____
_____
_____

3. To which one verse can you most readily relate? Why? _____
_____
_____
_____

David's life continually challenges us to answer questions such as:
- Am I becoming more and more committed to God?
- Do I have an increasing awareness that God is my rock, my fortress, and my deliverer?

Discovery

You will discover that God will always lead you to victory and He will lead you His way.

God does not play favorites. Anyone who cries out to Him, He answers. Anyone who surrenders to His call, He uses.

Addressing God personally and confidently comes from having an ongoing, intimate relationship with Him.

Addressing God personally and confidently comes from having an ongoing, intimate relationship with Him. Are you actively building a personal history with God? Can you honestly say that the two of you have done lots of living together since your salvation? Have you allowed God to reveal Himself to you in the many experiences of life?

If you are a Christian but you've attempted a life of self-sufficiency, you may not be able to relate to having a close personal relationship with God. Claiming Him personally is the most precious right of any believer!

The Father's deepest desire is to be loved—genuinely loved—by His child.

Write the first verse of Psalm 18. _____
_____
_____
_____

The One who delivered David from his enemies was no distant deity. He was the object of the psalmist's deepest emotions, the One with whom he shared an authentic relationship. David deeply loved God. The Father's deepest desire is to be loved—genuinely loved—by His child.

If 2 Samuel 22 and Psalm 18 force us to see one thing, it is that God is a personal God we each can call our own.
• He is my strength when I am weak.
• He is my rock when I am slipping.
• He is my deliverer when I am trapped.
• He is my fortress when I am crumbling.
• He is my Refuge when I am pursued.
• He is my Shield when I am exposed.
• He is my Lord when life spins out of control.

When has God shielded you from something that threatened you? Describe a particular time. _____
_____
_____
_____

When has God been your Deliverer? _____
_____
_____
_____

When has God been a Refuge when you felt like everyone needed more from you than you could give? _____
_____
_____
_____
_____

Meditation

Express your love for God by thanking Him for being your Shield, Deliverer, and Refuge. Acknowledge Him by these titles.

Satan always seeks to make us believe that God is unfair or unkind. To do this, Satan, the adversary, particularly likes to use a few difficult-to-understand events recorded in Scripture. This passage may be confusing and unsettling to us if we don't keep one thought in mind: We do not know every fact about every event in Scripture. We don't always have the explanations for certain events and acts of God. He is sovereign. He owes us no explanation. He is also obligated to teach us to walk by faith and not by sight. When Scripture records an event or judgment of God that seems cruel or unfair, we need to respond in the following two ways:

- We can acknowledge that His ways are higher than ours. We do not have all the information nor the understanding. We have no idea the depth of evil God may have seen in human hearts that demanded such serious judgment.
- We can acknowledge what we do know about God. Anytime you are overwhelmed by what you do not know or understand about God, consider what you do know about Him. Your heart and mind will find peace, and you will be able to walk in faith.

Read 2 Samuel 24:1-17.
According to verse 1, God's anger was directed to _____

Let's consider God's role in David's sin. The first verse of chapter 24 states, "He [God] incited David against them, saying, 'Go and take a census of Israel and Judah.'" A brief look at this one verse may cause us to wonder why God would ask David to do something and then kill 70,000 people as a result.

Just as God included four gospels to tell the story of the incarnate Christ, He recorded many of the occurrences of David's reign in both 2 Samuel and 1 Chronicles. We can better understand passages or events by comparing these "parallel" accounts.

First Chronicles 21:1 sheds a little light on what happened to David. What does this verse add to what you learned in 2 Samuel 24:1? _____
_____
_____
_____

How does James 1:13 shed light on our understanding of 2 Samuel 24:1 and 1 Chronicles 21:1? _____
_____
_____
_____

According to 1 Corinthians 10:13, what makes us vulnerable to temptation? ___
_____
_____

Scripture

David said to Gad, "I am in deep distress. Let us fall into the hands of the Lord, for his mercy is great; but do not let me fall into the hands of men" (2 Sam. 24:14).

God's ways are higher than our ways.

When you are overwhelmed by what you do not know or understand about God, consider what you do know about Him.

Discovery

You will discover that although you may not always understand everything that happens, God is sovereign—He is in control.

God never tempts us.

When we are tempted God always makes a way of escape.

From these two verses we know that God does not tempt us. He may allow us to be tempted to test, prove, or help us grow; but He is definitely not the tempter. In our temptation He always makes a way of escape. How do we explain the activity of God in David's sin? We can be assured that God did not tempt David to sin and then judge him harshly for it. God has no sin; therefore, He is incapable of enticing one to sin. He did, however, allow David to be tempted because He saw something in David's heart that needed to be exposed.

Consider the second matter Satan, the author of confusion and doubt, may use—the punishment seemed to exceed the crime. If we are not careful to study the text, 70,000 men seemed to die solely as a result of David's sin. Although David's actions no doubt displeased God and caused judgment, 2 Samuel 24:1 clearly states the anger of the Lord burned against Israel. We do not know why God's anger burned against Israel. What can we know in order to shed light on Israel's action that angered God?

1. The promise of God's blessing or cursing.

Read Deuteronomy 28:1-24. What can you conclude about the nature of Israel's sin against God that angered Him in 2 Samuel 24:1? _____
_____
_____

2. The tenderness of God.

In Exodus 32:25-30, what happened to those who were not for the Lord?
❑ **They were killed.**
❑ **They fled to the city of refuge.**
❑ **They were swallowed in the earth.**
❑ **They were rejected by the people of Israel.**

We don't know what Israel had done to make God so angry, but we do know His judgment was consistent with what He had promised for rebellion against His commands. Somehow Israel had severely disobeyed God. Why, then, was David also wrong? I'd like to suggest three possible reasons David was involved in the anger of God toward Israel.

1. He deserted the throne God had given him and did not trust God to fight his battles.
2. He did not stand in the gap and intercede for the sins of his nation as Moses did.
3. He possessed wrong motives for taking the census.

Based on 2 Samuel 24 and 1 Chronicles 21, David and the people of Israel shared the responsibility for the judgment handed down to them. In the heart of this difficult account of anger and judgment is something vital you must not miss—God's mercy.

Read 2 Samuel 24:18-25. What reason did David give Araunah for building the altar? Complete the following verse by filling in the missing words: "So I can build an altar to the Lord, that the _____" (v. 21).

When Araunah offered to give his threshing floor to David, how did David respond? Complete the following verse: "No, I insist on paying you for it. I will not sacrifice to the Lord my God burnt offerings that _____." (v. 24).

The threshing floor of Araunah the Jebusite was the most vital place in Israel's history. When the angel of the Lord stretched out his hand at the threshing floor, God seemed to cry. He "panted" in grief somewhat like one "being consoled over the death of an infant child."[1]

We now embark on the last lap of our journey with King David. We will enter the final years of his life and witness the succession of a new king. We will study his last public address and his personal advice to his son. We will reflect with him on the twists and turns of his eventful life and share in the wisdom he attained.

Read 1 Kings 1:1-27. Identify each of the following statements as either true or false.
____ **Adonijah was the son of David born after Absalom.**
____ **Bathsheba was Adonijah's mother.**
____ **Adonijah wanted to be the commander of the army in Joab's place.**
____ **Adonijah wanted to be king.**
____ **David had never questioned Adonijah's behavior.**

By the standards of his day, David was not an extremely old man. He was approaching his death at a far younger age than the patriarchs who preceded him. Perhaps his 70 years of active living could easily compare to 100 years of simply being alive. He had known virtually every extremity of the human experience—unparalleled success, unabashed rebellion, unashamed mourning, and uninhibited celebration. Life had taken its toll.

Years ago, God led me to write down my response to the extremities of life. I'd like to share these words with you.

> Satisfy me not with the lesser of You
> Find me no solace in shadows of the True
> No ordinary measure of extraordinary means
> The depth, the length, the breadth of You
> And nothing in between.
> Etch these words upon my heart, knowing all the while
> No ordinary roadblocks plague extraordinary miles
> Your power as my portion, Your glory as my fare
> Take me to extremities,
> But meet me fully there.

Mediation

Meditate on Exodus 34:6. When faced in Scripture with something that you don't understand and God seems cruel, remember how God identifies Himself: "... compassionate and gracious ... slow to anger, abounding in love and faithfulness."

Scripture

"You, my son Solomon, acknowledge the God of your father, and serve him with wholehearted devotion and with a willing mind, for the Lord searches every heart and understands every motive behind the thoughts. If you seek him, he will be found by you; but if you forsake him, he will reject you forever" (1 Chron. 28:9).

What do these words mean to you? _____

_____

_____

David lived most of his life in the extremes, but He met God at every venture. His roller coaster ride was nearing an end. The Psalms prove he had discovered God at every curve. I want my life to be like his. I don't want to make the mistakes he made, but I want to meet God at every high, every low, and every stop in between.

Need has a way of breathing fresh life into a soul, if just for a moment. David, who seemed chilled with the onset of death, assumes swift control, performs the will of God, and meets the desires of his queen's heart. Whether on his sickbed or on his throne, David was indeed still king.

Read 1 Kings 1:28-53. What words did Bathsheba say to David as she "bowed low with her face to the ground"? _____

_____

_____

The following statements are directions David gave to Zadok, Nathan, and Benaiah. Place them in proper order by numbering them one to four.

____ **Have Zadok and Nathan anoint Solomon king over Israel.**

____ **Blow the trumpet and shout, "Long live King Solomon!"**

____ **Set Solomon on my mule and take him to Gihon.**

____ **Seat Solomon on David's throne.**

A prophet, a priest, and a warrior were chosen to confirm the new king. For the nation to be strong, all four areas of authority needed to be present: prophet, priest, warrior, and king. Interestingly, our Lord and Savior Jesus Christ will ultimately fill every one of those positions. All authority has been given to Christ (Matt. 28:18)! Under one Head, all nations will finally be unified.

Describe David's response to the news of Solomon's anointing. _____

_____

_____

_____

We have seen many pivotal points in David's life. Now we come to one of the most significant turning points. He is passing the kingdom—from the hands of a shepherd to the hands of a businessman.

Solomon is not described like Absalom and Adonijah, handsome and obvious choices for a would-be king. God told Samuel, "The Lord does not look at the things man looks at. Man looks at the outward appearance, but the Lord looks at the heart" (1 Sam. 16:7). Solomon may not have been the natural choice in the eyes of men. He was not the oldest of the sons of David. Solomon represented God's divine mercy. He was the embodiment of second chances. He was the innocence that came from guilt. He was God's choice as history would prove.

I find enormous security in the consistency of God. He is always merciful. Christ Jesus would never have become flesh to dwell among us had it not been for man's scandalous sin. Jesus certainly did not display the image of the king Israel was expecting, yet He was the embodiment of second chances. He took our guilt on His innocent shoulders and became sin for us, so we could become the righteousness of God in Him (2 Cor. 5:21). Why? Because we were God's choice.

Do you have difficulty accepting yourself as God's good choice? ❏ Yes ❏ No Why or why not? _____

_____

_____

_____

Discovery

You will discover that God is always merciful.

David's rule ended just as it officially began. His stiffened body bowed before God on his final day as king, with the same abandon he demonstrated when he danced through the streets of Jerusalem. Wasn't it David who said, "Bless the Lord, O my soul: and all that is within me, bless his holy name." (Ps. 103:1, KJV)?

So we greet a new king. The first order of business for the new king was the building of a house for the Name of the Lord. Before he died the old king gathered the materials and drafted the plans for the work.

According to 1 Chronicles 22:5, why did David make preparations for the house to be built for the Lord?
❏ **He had no confidence in Solomon.**
❏ **Solomon asked him to make the preparations.**
❏ **Solomon was young and inexperienced.**
❏ **David wanted to be involved in the building of the temple.**

In 1 Chronicles 22:19 to what did David tell Solomon and the leaders of Israel to devote their hearts and souls? _____

_____

_____

In verses 14-16, David shared with Solomon all that had been gathered for the building of the sanctuary and all who had been commissioned to help. God provides what we need. We need to get busy.

How do the following two references suggest our need to "get busy"?

Ephesians 2:10 _____

_____

_____

David lived most of his life in the extremes, but He met God at every venture.

God is always merciful.

We are God's choice.

2 Timothy 3:16-17 _____

_____

_____

God promised His plans are to prosper us, to give us hope and a future (Jer. 29:11). The Word of God and Christ's indwelling Spirit equip us to fulfill the works preordained for us in God's perfect plan. Get busy!

God has placed concerns (burdens) in our hearts. These concerns function as a guide to show us the areas where God wants us to serve. In the Book of Matthew, Christ simplifies the process of finding our hearts and their attachments. He said, "Where your treasure is, there your heart will be also" (Matt. 6:21). Our hearts are attached to our treasure. So the question becomes, what is our treasure? Little awakens us to a realization of what we've treasured like turmoil and suffering. We find out quickly what our priorities have been.

Read 1 Chronicles 28:1-10.

Listen to David's strong and specific words to Solomon in verse 9: "You, my son Solomon, acknowledge the God of your father, and serve him with wholehearted devotion and with a willing mind, for the Lord searches every heart and understands every motive behind the thoughts. If you seek him, he will be found by you; but if you forsake him, he will reject you forever." His words to Solomon are pertinent to us in every area of potential success. David gave his son three vital directives we would be wise to obey:

1. Acknowledge God. Acknowledging God the first thing every morning transforms my day. The first step to victory is acknowledging the authority of God in our lives. I try to accept the words of Joshua 24:15 as a personal daily challenge: "If serving the Lord seems undesirable to you, then choose for yourselves this day whom you will serve, whether the gods your forefathers served beyond the River, or the gods of the Amorites, in whose land you are living. But as for me and my household, we will serve the Lord."

God provides what we need. We need to get busy.

What does acknowledging God mean to you? How do you acknowledge God in your life? _____

_____

_____

_____

2. Serve Him with wholehearted devotion.

Do you have a divided heart? Does God have a piece of your heart, but the rest belongs to you? Or does your heart belong to someone else? _____

_____

_____

_____

A divided heart places our entire lives in jeopardy. Only God can be totally trusted with our hearts. David learned the price of a divided heart the hard way. He lived with the repercussions for the rest of his life. But David was also used of God to describe whole-hearted devotion. In Psalm 86:11 David asked of God, "Teach me your way, O Lord, and I will walk in your truth; give me an undivided heart, that I may fear your name."

3. *Serve Him with a willing spirit.* God wants us to serve Him and honor Him because we want to. Because it pleases us. Because we choose to! You see, the Lord searches every heart and understands every motive behind the thoughts.

Many motives exist for serving God other than pleasure. What are other reasons a person might serve God? _____
_____
_____
_____

God wants us to serve Him with a willing spirit, one that would choose no other way. Right now you may be frustrated because serving and knowing God is not your greatest pleasure. You may be able to instantly acknowledge a divided heart. Your question may be, How can I change the way I feel? You can't. But God can. Give Him your heart—your whole heart. Give Him permission to change it. The words of Deuteronomy 30:6 have changed my life and my heart.

Read Deuteronomy 30:6. Turn the verse into a personal prayer for a heart wholly devoted to God.

W e now witness the conclusion of David's address to the assembly. Notice he formally and publicly acknowledged God's sovereignty over Israel. He finalized plans and made preparations for the temple. He lifted prayers for a new king. David's final duties toward his beloved nation teach us new truths and recapture some of the most important lessons from the life of the shepherd king.

Solomon lacked nothing but age and experience—something that probably scared his father half to death! So David looked at the whole assembly and basically said, "Give him a hand. He's going to need it." Let's join the massive assembly now and hear the conclusion of David's address to the nation of Israel.

" Yours, O Lord, is the kingdom; you are exalted as head over all " (1 Chron. 29:11).

Read 1 Chronicles 29:1-9. What do you think motivated the leaders to give so freely? _____
_____
_____

According to verse 9, why did the people rejoice? _____
_____
_____

Never underestimate the power of a positive example!

Never underestimate the power of a positive example! David could not motivate the leaders of Israel to give freely and wholeheartedly to the Lord unless he gave. He could force them, but the willing spirit God so deeply desired would be forfeited. Their cheerful giving would be motivated by his own; therefore, he had to give more than what belonged to the kingdom. The third verse clearly tells us, "I now give my personal treasures of gold and silver for the temple of my God, over and above everything I have provided for this holy temple."

A divided heart places our entire lives in jeopardy. Only God can be totally trusted with our hearts.

Has a leader in your life ever motivated you to give your time, talents, gifts, or treasures as a result of his or her own example? ❑ Yes ❑ No **Who was the leader and how has his or her example affected you?** _____

_____

_____

_____

Read 1 Chronicles 29:10-20. Consider verses 10-13 carefully. Describe in one sentence what you believe David was saying. _____

_____

_____

_____

In 1 Chronicles 28:9, David told Solomon to serve God with wholehearted devotion. In 1 Chronicles 29:19, David asked God to give Solomon wholehearted devotion. The wholehearted devotion of a person toward God is obviously a joint work between God and the individual.

Don't ever forget the awesome benefits of authentic praise. God desires our praises for many reasons, but I believe among the most vital are these two:

1. Praise reminds us of who He is.
When I am overwhelmed and wonder if God can carry me through the storm, He often calls on me to claim out loud—before His ears and mine—some of His many virtues:
• His wonders in the lives of those recorded in the Word.
• His wonders in my own life.
• His wonders in the lives of those I know.

2. Praise reminds us of who we are.

Read Psalm 8:1-4. What caused David to gain a fresh perspective? _____

_____

_____

_____

_____

Our study has shown us the very best of a man's heart and the very worst. David's heart was the origin of his greatest delight and his gravest disaster.

In light of all we've learned together, do you see the extreme importance of watching over your heart and giving it wholly to the One who created you? ❑ Yes ❑ No If so, write a prayer of commitment, naming specific ways you will commit to keeping your heart in check. Be courageous in your prayer. Ask God to reveal every impurity in your heart as it first develops. _____

_____

_____

_____

_____

_____

Read 1 Chronicles 29:21-25. How did Solomon's kingdom compare to David's based on verse 25? _____

_____

_____

_____

_____

Discovery

You will discover that to serve God you must be totally devoted to Him.

In Psalm 69:16 David wrote: "Answer me, O Lord, out of the goodness of your love; in your great mercy turn to me." As his life comes to its end, we see how God graciously answered David.

The unrelenting sword was finally at rest. David's house was in order. God had given a weary man strength and helped him prepare a family and a nation for life in his absence. Surely as he bowed on his sickbed, David had prayed the words of Psalm 71:9.

David's heart was the origin of his greatest delight and his gravest disaster.

Write Psalm 71:9. _____

_____

_____

_____

_____

_____

_____

Read Psalm 71:14. What would David always have that no one could take from him? _____

_____

_____

Read Psalm 71:20 carefully. What hope did David have in the face of death? ___

_____

_____

_____

Read 1 Chronicles 29:26-30.

The God whose faithfulness endures to all generations completed the good work He started in a shepherd boy.

David has been a worthy subject for our study. The last words of 1 Chronicles read, "As for the events of King David's reign, from beginning to end, they are written in the records of Samuel the seer, the records of Nathan the prophet and the records of Gad the seer, together with the details of his reign and power, and the circumstances that surrounded him and Israel and the kingdoms of all the other lands" (1 Chron. 29:29-30).

God did not cast David away. God did not forsake him when he was old. The God whose faithfulness endures to all generations completed the good work He started in a shepherd boy. Now the work was finally finished.

"Then David rested with his fathers and was buried in the City of David" (1 Kings 2:10). The eyes that had peeked into the heart of God now closed in death. The earthly life of one of the most passionate and controversial figures ever to live ended. The deadly silence must have lasted only long enough for Bathsheba to place her ear close to his mouth and her hand on his heart. The faint rise and fall of his chest had ceased.

No doubt the silence gave way to wails of grief. Trumpets carried the news. A kind of mourning peculiar to the Hebrew nation filled the days that followed. The very instruments commissioned by David for the dedication of the temple ironically may have first played his funeral dirge. Multitudes heaped ashes on their heads and draped sackcloth on their bodies. After an intense period of national mourning with visits from foreign dignitaries, life continued—just as it has the audacity to do after we've lost a loved one.

Life went on, but forever marked by the life of God's chosen king. God sovereignly chose to chisel David's reign into a kingdom that would last forever.

As we close our study, read the words of Jeremiah 33:14-22. How certain is the covenant God made with David? _____
_____

Read Luke 2:4-7. What do these verses reveal? _____
_____
_____
_____
_____

Write Luke 1:32. _____
_____
_____
_____
_____
_____
_____

The distant grandson David wrote about in Psalm 110 was no surprise to David. God whispered these truths in his spirit and caused him to write them down for all eternity.

Read David's words in Psalm 110 aloud—hopefully with a fresh revelation of their significance! What did David call Christ in verse 1? _____

_____

Meditation

Reflect on what you've learned during this study. Pray for the Holy Spirit to remind you of specific truths about the heart.

Indeed, one unexpected day the clouds will roll back and the King of all kings will burst through the sky. "On that day his feet will stand on the Mount of Olives, east of Jerusalem, and the Mount of Olives will be split in two from east to west, forming a great valley, with half of the mountain moving north and half moving south. You will flee by my mountain valley, for it will extend to Azel. You will flee as you fled from the earthquake in the days of Uzziah king of Judah. Then the Lord my God will come, and all the holy ones with him. On that day there will be no light, no cold or frost. It will be a unique day, without daytime or nighttime—a day known to the Lord. When evening comes, there will be light. … The Lord will be king over the whole earth. On that day there will be one Lord, and his name the only name (Zech. 14:4-7,9).

Christ Jesus will sit on the throne of David in the city of Jerusalem and hope will give birth to certainty! We will join the one who said, "You turned my wailing into dancing; you removed my sackcloth and clothed me with joy, that my heart may sing to you and not be silent. O Lord my God, I will give you thanks forever" (Ps. 30:11-12). With David, we will sing to One who is worthy!

That day there just might be one who can't seem to stop singing. Oh, yes, I believe David will dance once more down the streets of Jerusalem. He will be oblivious to anyone but God, the passion of his heart. David will dance his way to that same familiar throne, but this time it will be occupied by Another. No one above Him. None beside Him. David will see the Lord high and lifted up and His train will fill the temple (see Isa. 6). He'll fall before the One who sits upon the throne, take the crown from his own head and cast it at His feet. He'll lift his eyes to the King of all kings and with the passions of an entire nation gathered in one heart, he will cry, "Worthy!"

What is the most significant way God has spoken to you through this study?

_____

_____

_____

Surely God the Father will look with great affection upon the pair.
All wrongs made right. All faith now sight.
He'll search the soul of a shepherd boy once more
And perhaps He will remark
How very much he has
A heart like His.

[1]Spiros Zodhiates, *The Complete Word Study Old Testament* (Chattanooga: AMG Publishers, 1994), 2340.